COMPANION
TO
EARLY MIDDLE ENGLISH LITERATURE

COMPANION
TO
EARLY MIDDLE ENGLISH LITERATURE

edited by

N.H.G.E. VELDHOEN

and

H. AERTSEN

Second, enlarged edition

VU UNIVERSITY PRESS

Amsterdam 1995

The illustration on the cover shows the text of *Havelok the Dane*, lines 632-53, from MS Laud Misc. 108, fol. 207v, in the Bodleian Library, Oxford.

VU University Press is an imprint of:
VU Boekhandel/Uitgeverij bv
De Boelelaan 1105
1081 HV Amsterdam
The Netherlands

tel. (0)20 - 644 43 55
fax (0)20 - 646 27 19

isbn 90-5383-349-8

PREFACE TO THE SECOND EDITION

The editors are happy to announce that the success of the first edition has made it possible to augment the second edition of this *Companion* by including three more essays; two from the original Leiden collection, and a new one from Utrecht. We expect that the usefulness of this volume has been enhanced by the coverage of a larger range of early Middle English texts.

This first edition can be used alongside the first, since nothing from the first edition has been left out. Most of the errors in the first edition, however, have been corrected, and the lay-out has been brought in line with what has now become a series of Companions.

University of Leiden   N.H.G.E. Veldhoen
Vrije Universiteit, Amsterdam   H. Aertsen
December, 1994

FROM THE PREFACE TO THE FIRST EDITION

The essays in this collection are introductions to a number of widely-read early Middle English texts, aimed at students who are coming to these texts with little experience of reading Middle English other than Chaucer. The purpose in each case is to stimulate a critical engagement by providing a literary approach and some historical context. Text-historical and linguistic analyses fall outside the scope of this book.

This collection of essays can be used alongside many anthologies of Middle English literature. References to texts are always to standard editions wherever possible.

This volume is a Dutch production: the authors and editors are, or were, all teaching at various universities in the Netherlands. Some of the contributions were originally written for a similar collection that circulated for a few years as an internal publication of the English Department of the University of Leiden.

University of Leiden   N.H.G.E. Veldhoen
Free University, Amsterdam   H. Aertsen
July, 1988

CONTENTS

1 The Middle English Lyrics: An Introduction
   ALASDAIR A. MACDONALD   7

2 *St Kenelm* and the Legends of the English Saints in
   the *South English Legendary*
   RENEE HAMELINCK   19

3 *Havelok the Dane*: A Non-Courtly Romance
   HENK AERTSEN   29

4 *Floris and Blauncheflour*: To Indulge the Fancy and
   to Hear of Love
   N.H.G.E. VELDHOEN   51

5 *Dame Sirith* and *De Clerico et Puella*
   KEITH BUSBY   67

6 *The Fox and the Wolf*: A Study in Medieval Irony
   WIM TIGGES   79

7 *The Land of Cokaygne*: Sophisticated Mirth
   WIM TIGGES   93

8 Life, Lore, and Logic in *The Owl and the Nightingale*
   JUDITH C. PERRYMAN   103

9 The Twofold Harmony of the Middle English *Sir Orfeo*
   ERIK KOOPER   115

10 *The Ancrene Wisse*
   JOHAN KERLING   133

THE MIDDLE ENGLISH LYRICS
AN INTRODUCTION

ALASDAIR A. MACDONALD
(University of Groningen)

A glance through any anthology of medieval literature suffices to reveal that, in those remote centuries, verse was a possible medium for many literary kinds for which the modern writer would naturally use prose (for example, sermons, histories, tales of adventure, philosophical disquisitions). Most of the poetry composed today is of the lyric sort, of which the more obvious characteristics are brevity, subjectivity, use of metaphor and symbol, registration and expression of strong emotions, and—as traditional formal features—stanzas, rhyme and regular rhythm. The difference between medieval and modern custom entrains two immediate consequences: first, we may find it difficult to consider the verse of lengthy romances and chronicles as, in a sense, real poetry; and second, when we encounter specimens of the medieval lyric we are liable to a pleasant shock of recognition which may be not quite warranted. While one may choose to see in the medieval lyric the beginning of a great tradition which continues to the present, one must be prepared also to make allowance for not a few points of difference.

Lyric poetry in English was one of the great innovations of the Middle Ages. But one naturally wonders first whether there are any connections with Old English verse. Although Anglo-Saxon poets were capable of expressing thoughts and feelings in memorable and rather special ('lyrical') language, they seem scarcely to have used the formal devices which later became so common. *Deor* and *Wulf and Eadwacer* might perhaps be said to use stanzas, and *The Riming Poem* and such pieces as the *Chronicle* poem on Alfred the Atheling (1036) show that rhyme was not unknown. Yet these very devices mark out such poems as exceptions in the Old English tradition, and Pearsall (1977:73; also, 70-74) has dismissed *The Riming Poem* as a "lunatic exercise". In some of the poems preserved in *The Anglo-Saxon Chronicle*, however, there is a trend towards unclassically regular two-stress rhythms and rhyme, which looks forward to such works as Laȝamon's *Brut* and *The Proverbs of Alfred*. The earliest Middle English lyrics for which music has survived, the songs of St Godric (d. 1170), show this kind of transitional writing, which seems to be moving towards stanza, rhyme and rhythm, but which is still organized on the basis of half-lines and employs alliteration, albeit of a rather attenuated type:

> Sainte Nicholas,   Godes druð,
> tymbre us faiere   scoone hus.
> At þi burðe,   at þi bare,
> Sainte Nicholas,   bring us wel þare.
>   (*MES*, 103)

> (St Nicholas, beloved of God, prepare for us beautiful and lovely dwelling-places. Through the merits of thy birth and of thy death, bring us, St Nicholas, there in safety.)

By the thirteenth century, however, regular rhythm, rhyme and stanzas are firmly established, and alliteration, though it can still be important, is used in lyric verse not as a structural, but as a decorative feature.

The antecedents of the stanza-forms used in England in the Middle English lyric lie not in the native tradition, but in the Latin tradition of hymnody, which goes back to the Office hymns of St Ambrose (d. 397). There we find regularity of stanza and rhythm, and often rhyme as well. These Latin lyrics, well-known from constant use in church, exercised an enormous influence on the vernacular verse of Western Europe. Latin poems were themselves also influenced by vernacular song, and in all periods the religious and the secular lyrics remain closely in touch with one another (see Dronke, 1978:32-85). After the Norman Conquest, three languages were used for lyric verse in England: Latin, Anglo-Norman, and English. Not surprisingly, we find texts in which there appear, side by side, poems in all three tongues, and also lyrics in which there is a mixture of languages. In Bodleian MS Douce 139 there occurs the following brief definition of love:

> Loue is a selkud wodenesse
> Þat þe idel mon ledeth by wildernesse,
> Þat þurstes of wilfulscipe and drinket sorwenesse
> And with lomful sorwes menget his blithnesse.
>   (*CB.XIII*, 14-15)

> (Love is an extraordinary madness, which leads the idle man through the wilderness, so that he thirsts after pleasure and drinks sorrow, and mingles his joy with continual griefs.)

These lines are accompanied by Latin and French versions of the same: *Amor est quedam mentis insania* etc., and *Amur est une pensee enragee* etc. With the texts of some poems—for example, *Eyns ne soy ke pleynte fu / Ar ne kuth ich sorghe non* ('Formerly I knew no sorrow'; *MES*, 110-111; *CB.XIII*, 10-13)—each of the English lines is given below its French counterpart (the French lines themselves follow musical notation): in this case the English is a reworking (*contrafactum*) of the French, and is to be sung to the same tune. However, behind the French words is a previous Latin poem of the type known as 'sequence', in which the stanzas, though they may vary the one from the other, nevertheless fall into two identically constructed halves. The English words of *Sumer is icumen in* (*MES*, 143; *CB.XIII*, 13), on the other hand, are found in BL MS Harley 978 *above* those in Latin, but, as Dobson and Harrison convincingly argue, this stems from the practical need to make the lines fill the allotted space, and does not imply prior composition in English (which, though possible, would be exceptional).

Whereas in the thirteenth century the exigencies of Latin musical forms frequently dictated the form of the resulting English poems, later in the medieval period lyrics were often purely literary creations, not based on pre-existing songs. Among the more celebrated specimens of this type of lyric may be mentioned the series of refrain poems from the Vernon MS, Bodleian MS Eng. poet. a.1 (*CB. XIV*, 125-208; Pearsall, 1977:140-43). Throughout the history of the Middle English lyric, the influence from both Latin and French models, musical and literary, sacred and secular, continued to be felt. With the eventual decline in the use of Anglo-Norman, however, the English lyrics gained in independence—although the Chaucerian poets were much obliged to Continental French models. For its part, the influence of Latin in the fourteenth to sixteenth centuries was no longer mainly at the level of form, but rather at that of content and expression.

The Middle English religious lyrics outnumber their secular counterparts by a ratio of about five to one. A number of reasons may be given for this. Since today we have only what has been written down, we can have little idea of what would have appealed to the taste of the illiterate majority of the population, should that have differed from the taste of the literate minority. To speak of medieval folksongs is very risky, while 'popular' song or verse could well have appealed (as today) to all classes of society and to all levels of education. Another factor is that of chance survival: we have no sure grounds for assuming that the extant remains are truly representative of the entire

corpus of lyrics. Furthermore, we are at the mercy of the copyists.
Most English lyrics are found in manuscripts linked with monasteries
or other religious houses, and we may surmise that the scribes and
authors were monks, priests, friars, or, at the least, clerics in minor
orders. Although it would be rash to assume that the tastes of these
men were necessarily narrow, it is obvious that religious material,
which was officially approved, would stand the best chance of being
preserved. Many secular lyrics, indeed, are known only from chance
scribblings in the margins of more 'respectable' works.

Interpretation and critical appreciation of the Middle English
lyrics makes desirable our knowing something about the identity of
the authors, the occasions for which the poems were composed, the
opportunities for performance, the functions the poems were intended
to have, and the rhetorical means by which these functions were
effected. It is, of course, possible to dispense with these preparatives,
and to approach the poems 'blind'. With unfamiliar art forms, however, there is little chance that an immediate response—be it ever so
sincerely or strongly felt—will be very helpful. Moreover, the modern
reader may have to disabuse himself of hand-me-down critical
assumptions—such as a tendency to generalise about 'medievalism'
and to find it romantic, or to consider the lyrics as evincing charming
naivety, rugged simplicity, primitive purity, of any combination
thereof. The critic may indeed find certain lyrics charming, or simple,
or primitive, but his finding will take its value from the appreciation
of the context in which the poems belong. This problem of critical
interference bedevils the study of the lyrics more than that of other
medieval works or genres because of the treacherous continuity in the
composition of the lyrics, and because it has sometimes been
supposed that a medieval lyric can be adequately approached as if it
had been composed yesterday. Edith Sitwell (1972:245) described
Maid in the moor lay (*MES*, 188-189) as a 'miracle of poetry': the
phrase perhaps suggests more about her conception of poetry than it
illuminates the medieval work itself.

The biographical approach is not of much help to the student of
Middle English lyrics, since so little is known about even those few
poets whose names are recorded. The obscurity does not mean,
however, that the poems were the spontaneous or long-evolved
creations of an anonymous 'folk'. Rather, the obscurity is the result of
accidental losses of information, on the one hand, and, on the other,
the fact that, from the outset, the lyrics were intended for general use
and were not conceived as the expression of the unique thoughts and

experiences of particular individuals, recollected in conditions of more or less tranquillity. It is possible, nonetheless, to say something about the authors' background and the cultural milieu in which they were working. The very use of the English language suggests that the intended audience was the ordinary people: the priests had their Latin, and the Court (until the fifteenth century) its French. The religious lyrics can be seen as giving poetic expression to the tasks of quickening and propagating the faith, and their survival is a measure of their success. The secular lyrics—of which the great majority would also be the work of clerics—similarly reach out to please their English-speaking audience.

It is especially (though not exclusively) the Franciscan friars who are associated with the religious lyrics: for example, Thomas of Hales (c. 1275), William Herebert (d. 1333), John Grimestone (c. 1372), James Ryman (late fifteenth century). Unlike the monks, the friars travelled widely among the people, frequently preached in the open air at preaching-crosses, and were even regarded as competitors by the parish priests. In their sermons they often made use of vernacular verse, and several of the manuscripts which preserve Middle English lyrics are, in fact, anthologies assembled by friars (Pearsall, 1977:132-40; Wenzel, 1978:61-132; Wilson, 1973:vii-xvi). The role of the Franciscans in the religious lyric is also borne out by the manuscripts, which show many shared items. This permits one to conclude that the best lyrics must have been circulated by the friars in their travels. Of all types of religious lyric the most popular was indubitably the carol, and R.L. Greene has discussed the important part played by the Franciscans in the composition, transcription and dissemination of such pieces (1977:cl-clvii). In one lyric (not a carol) in Bodleian MS Digby 2 (*CB.XIII*, 126) we find the line, *Frer menur I wil me make*: this is—one must assume—the putative resolution of one who had already joined the order. In fact, in the history of the Middle English lyrics one can hardly overemphasize the contribution made by the friars.

The church liturgy was, of course, conducted in Latin, but there were plenty opportunities for the extraliturgical use of religious lyrics: for example, in the course of sermons, during processions, during banquets, in the speeches of characters in religious dramas, and in optional musical fragments, such as the substitution of vernacular pieces for the often sung phrase, *Benedicamus domino*. Other lyrics would have been used in the private devotions of individuals. Many so-called lyrics are humble versifications of the *Pater Noster*, *Ave Maria* or

Credo, with few literary pretensions. Other lyrics—listing such things as the joys and sorrows (five, seven, or fifteen) of Our Lady, or the various headings under which sins might be confessed (the five wits, the seven deadly sins, the seven deeds of corporal and spiritual mercy, the seven sacraments, the ten commandments, the twelve articles of faith, etc.)—doubtless owed their popularity to their mnemonic usefulness. Again, the subject-matter of many religious lyrics may be connected with the festivals of the church year (for example, the Annunciation, Nativity, Passion and Resurrection), and it is important to take this context into account. While it would be naive to suppose that medieval congregations did not understand what regular iteration had made familiar to them in the Latin of the church services, they would presumably respond with greater immediacy to devotional texts in their own language, and which were not restricted to use in church. It is no accident that the greatly increased composition of religious lyrics in the fourteenth, fifteenth and early sixteenth centuries coincides with the growth of devotions with a wide appeal (for example, to the Holy Name, the Five Wounds, the Rosary), and with the use in manuscript and printed Books of Hours of iconographic figures (for example, the *imago pietatis*, Christ displaying the wounds of the Crucifixion; the *arma Christi*, the instruments of the Passion; the mass of St Gregory, illustrating the miraculous power of the Eucharist) which could be 'imprinted' on the imagination, in order to stimulate meditation. The later Middle Ages, furthermore, witnessed a remarkable development of Marian devotion, and this is clearly reflected in the enthusiasm for lyrics on this theme (Woolf, 1968:274-308, 389-91; Gray, 1972:18-30). Yet another factor to be borne in mind is that the religious lyrics in the case of versifications of approved prayer texts were often associated with indulgences: this was a sure passport to popularity in the eschatologically-minded later Middle Ages. For example, the lyric, *Haill Mary, quhais concepcioun*, is a rendering of the Latin verses, *Ave cuius concepcio*, which was one of the commonest items in Books of Hours; this prayer carried an indulgence from Pope Sixtus IV, in the terms of which the length of time spent in Purgatory by the soul of the person devoutly saying the prayer was reduced by 11000 years (Bennett, 1955:xx-xxi). An awareness of the devotional practices of medieval society thus greatly helps one to understand why religious lyrics were written, and what purposes they were designed to serve.

Two brief illustrations may be given of the continuing appeal, but also the textual problems, of the Middle English lyrics. The thirteenth-century poem *Of on þat is so fayr and briȝt*, from BL MS Egerton 613 (*CB.XIII*, 26-7), was rearranged to make the later lyric *A lady þat was so feyre & briȝt* (Bodleian MS Ashmole 1393; fifteenth century; *CB.XV*, 34-5). Both mingle short lines of English with lines consisting of familiar Latin religious tags. The earlier poem has forty-five lines, in nine-line stanzas. In the later poem these are trimmed to twenty-eight lines in four-line stanzas (and survive with music). Though a great deal is shared between the two poems, there is a perceptible change in emphasis. Whereas in the first version we find a loving wonderment at Mary's role in the miraculous scheme of salvation, in the second there is a sharper focus on the honour which she thereby deserves. The later version ends thus:

> Of all wymmen þu berist þe price,
>   *mater generosa*,
> Grawnt vs all paradys,
>   *virgo gloriosa*.
>   (*CB.XV*, 35)

> (Of all women you are the most excellent, noble mother, grant all of us access to Paradise, exalted virgin.)

This is a revision of a pair of lines which appear near the middle of the earlier version, but the use of the lines as conclusion quite changes the impact. As a result of such modifications a tighter, more effective poem has been produced.

The second example is provided by the celebrated fifteenth-century *I syng of a myden* (i.e. maiden; *CB.XV*, 119), which uses lines from the poem *Nu þis fules singet* (*CB.XIII*, 55):

> I syng of a myden   þat is makeles,
> kyng of alle kynges   to here sone che ches.
> he cam also stylle   þer his moder was
> as dew in aprylle,   þat fallyt on þe gras.
> he cam also stylle   to his moderes bowr
> as dew in aprille,   þat fallyt on þe flour.
> he cam also stylle   þer his moder lay
> as dew in aprille,   þat fallyt on þe spray.
> moder & mayden was neuer non but che—
> wel may swych a lady godes moder be.
>   (*CB.XV*, 119)

(I sing of a maiden, peerless, without stain: she chose the king of
all kings as her son. He came so softly where his mother was, like
dew in April falling on the grass. He came so softly to his mother's
chamber, like dew in April falling on the flower. He came so softly
where his mother lay, like dew in April falling on the blossom.
None but she was ever mother and maiden: such a lady can truly be
the Mother of God.)

The scriptural basis of the two poems is the account of the Annunciation in St Luke's gospel (i:26-38), and also the text of Isaiah (xiv:8)
which uses the image of dew as a figuration of the divine grace which
falls on the earth. It is small wonder that the latter text is much quoted
in the liturgy during the period of Advent, just before the celebration
of the birth of Christ. The earlier poem shows the scriptural narrative
recast into fairly straightforward verse, whereas the later one shows a
real poetic power which derives from the total concentration on the
central metaphor of dew, with its obvious connotations of beauty,
moisture, purity and fertility, together with the slow disclosure of the
initial mystery as one comes gradually to realise the identity of the
maiden. *Nu þis fules singet* retells the paradox; *I syng of a myden*
enacts it. The success of the later poem has nothing to do with novelty
of thought, but everything to do with artistic control over expression.

   Wen þe turuf is þi tuur (*CB.XIII*, 54) is a lyric which clearly
shows the need for criticism of medieval poetry to begin with an
appreciation of the medieval context—in this case the literature of
courtly love:

> Wen þe turuf is þi tuur,
> & þi put is þi bour,
> þi wel & þi wite þrote
> ssulen wormes to note.
> Wat helpit þe þenne
> al þe worilde wnne?
> (*CB.XIII*, 54)

(When the turf is your tower and your grave your bedchamber,
your skin and your white throat shall be food for worms. What will
it help you then, all the profit of the world?)

The method of the poet here is to contrast sharply the 'tower' (of the
castle of love, of safety in the pride of life) and the 'bower' (of
intimate erotic and social intercourse) with the grim physical reality of
the 'turf' and 'pit' (of the grave). Love and death, transience and eter-

nity, light and darkness, warmth and chill, the delights of the human imagination and the ineluctable conditions of human existence—these are the antinomies which the poem evokes, and the use of alliteration forces one to consider both terms of the stark contrasts. The brevity of the poem allows the reader no escape from the intended *frisson*: he must recognise that the foundations of his behaviour and values are as shadows in the light of eternal verities. It is good that the lyric ends with the challenge of the rhetorical question. The unspoken answer is clear, though men may choose to forget it: to spell it out would be unnecessary, and poetically disastrous. In this lyric the author's artistic discretion brilliantly succeeds in communicating his message, yet, after this is understood in terms of the medieval vision of life, we can see that the poem has also achieved a power to affect which is universal. As with many other early Middle English lyrics, one of the chief poetic successes of this piece (which is actually a translation from Latin) is a laconic expression which makes the lines seem pregnant with meaning. At its best it is an art of concentration.

The very important BL MS Harley 2253 bears out most of what has been said above. It contains prose and verse, lyrics and longer poems, Latin, French and English. One or two lyrics, indeed, use all three languages—as in this stanza, which concludes a macaronic lyric presumably composed by a student-cleric at the University of Paris:

Scripsi hec carmina in tabulis;
mon ostel est en mi la vile de Paris;
may y sugge namore, so wel me is;
ȝef hi deȝe for loue of hire, duel hit ys.
(*HL*, 55)

(I have written these verses in my will; my lodging is in the middle of the city of Paris; I can say no more, so great is my good fortune; if I die for love of her, it will be a grievous sorrow.)

The manuscript, taken as a whole, clearly reflects the learned tastes of the compilers, and the poem just quoted is evidently the work of a thirteenth-century 'university wit'. Such people would be quite likely to import into English poetry French (Provençal and Northern) literary fashions, such as, within the general European craze for courtly love, the *reverdie* (a song of Spring), the *chanson d'aventure* (a light-hearted narrative of love), and the *pastourelle* (a variant of the previous, involving a knight and a female social inferior, often in a woodland setting).

The variety of dialect features displayed by the Harley lyrics shows that many of them originated outside the West Midlands, where they were collected by some churchman, perhaps in Leominster, near Hereford. The special importance of this Harley text lies in the number of delightful secular lyrics which it preserves, although these are only a small proportion of the total contents of the manuscript. If one remembers the even more celebrated medieval collection, the *Carmina Burana*, one will not be surprised that love poems so appealed in ecclesiastical circles. One lyric, *My deþ y loue* (*CB.XIII*, 152-4; *HL*, 62-3), shows a clerical lover at work, charming his victim into a surrender which is far from undesired; the testimony of the Wife of Bath confirms the appeal of such *glosing* (Chaucer *WB* 509).

Another Harley poem, *Mosti ryden by Rybbesdale* (*HL*, 37-9), consists mainly of an itemised list of the lady's attractions, and there is a charming physicality (somewhat in the manner of Robert Herrick) in the lines. This allows of easy visualisation: one will remember the grey eyes, the arching brows, the whalebone-white teeth, the skin whiter than morning-fresh milk. The poet fantasises about riding through Ribblesdale (in Lancashire) to choose one of the *'wilde wymmen'*, but the lady of his choice is praised in courtly terms. Her red lips are ideal for reading romances (*romaunz forte rede*), and the climax of the poem wittily plays on the conjunction of a heavenly and earthly paradise:

> He myhte sayen þat Crist hym seȝe
> þat myhte nyhtes neh hyre leȝe,
>   heuene he heuede here.
>
>   (*HL*, 39)

(He could say that Christ was watching over him; he who could lie at night beside her would be enjoying heaven here.)

The lady's breasts are *as apples tuo of Parays* (i.e. Paradise), and the poet would choose to watch for her coming, rather than *beon pope ant ryde in Rome*. The hyperbolical nature of many of the compliments contained in the poem is typical of medieval clerical wit.

The tone and expression of a lyric are not predetermined by the subject-matter, although they will naturally be influenced by it. There are many things to say about love and many ways of saying them, and this variety applies no less to religious subjects. What counts is the coordination of form—whether song, narrative, prayer, exposition, invective, mnemonic or meditation—with the affective purpose in-

tended. The early lyric, *Nou goth sonne vnder wod* (*CB.XIII*, 1), found
with the Passion meditation for sext (Mary's commission to St John)
in the *Speculum Ecclesiae* of St Edmund of Abingdon (d. 1240), and
William Dunbar's *Amang thir freiris, within ane cloister* (late fif-
teenth/early sixteenth century) are both personal meditations on the
Passion, yet, whereas the former is justly celebrated for its tremendous
understatement, the latter contains a brutally pictorial narrative of the
sufferings of Christ, followed by an account in allegorical terms of the
effect upon the meditator (in Kinsley, 1979:7-11). The differences
between the two poems are enormous; yet, though the juxtaposition
reveals two radically different conceptions of religious lyric poetry,
the underlying function of the lyrics is similar. One could likewise
oppose the simple, fourteenth-century lyric from the school of Richard
Rolle, *Lo! lemman swete, now may þou se* (*CB.XIV*, 94), with the
early sixteenth-century lyric, *O man remember and prent in to þi
thocht*, of William Stewart (*Bannatyne MS*, ii.90-95). In each poem,
Christ asks man to remember what He has suffered for him. The first
concludes with all the tenderness of divine love:

> And, swete lemman, forget þow noght
> þat I þi lufe sa dere haue boght,
> And I aske þe noght elles.
> (*CB.XIV*, 94)

> (And forget not, sweet loved-one, that I so dearly have bought your
> love, and I ask nothing else from you.)

The second, however, is the work of a stern moralist, and the refrain
which Stewart puts into the mouth of Christ has a distinctly threat-
ening ring to it: *Amend thy mis, this plaig sall pas the fra* ('reform
your sinful life, and this plague shall leave you'). For most types of
lyrics, sacred and secular, one could probably find a commensurately
wide range of expressive possibilities.

The period of the medieval English lyric extends from the
twelfth to the early sixteenth centuries, and an evolution along the
way is only to be expected. Among the qualities of the early Middle
English lyric may be remarked an engaging freshness in the love
poems and a dense brevity in the religious poems. In later centuries
one sees a greater use of rhetorical colours, a growing elaboration of
stanza forms, an increasing love of latinate vocabulary (aureate
terms), and a tendency for the lyrics to discard the anonymity of their
predecessors. Yet these trends were not exclusive, and there are mas-

terly lyrics and carols in the simple style in the fifteenth century. The Middle English lyric is not a monolithic phenomenon, but a richly diverse art form which was continually developing. Though many of these poems achieve a universality of appeal which may speak to us across the centuries, they all benefit from a critical approach which tries to see them against the cultural background on which they drew and of which they are an expression.

ABBREVIATED TITLES

Bannatyne MS. :: *The Bannatyne MS.* Ed. W. Tod Ritchie. 4 Vols. Scottish Text Society. Edinburgh and London. 1928-34.
CB.XIII :: *English Lyrics of the Thirteenth Century.* Ed. C. Brown. Oxford: O.U.P. 1932.
CB.XIV :: *Religious Lyrics of the Fourteenth Century.* Ed. C. Brown. 2nd ed. rev. G.V. Smithers. Oxford: O.U.P. 1957.
CB.XV :: *Religious Lyrics of the Fifteenth Century.* Ed. C. Brown. Oxford: O.U.P. 1939.
Chaucer *WB*. In: *The Works of Geoffrey Chaucer.* Ed. F.N. Robinson. 2nd ed. Boston, MA: Houghton Mifflin [Cambridge, MA: Riverside Press], and London: O.U.P. 1957. (1st ed., 1933.)
HL :: *The Harley Lyrics.* Ed. G.L. Brook. 4th ed. Manchester: Manchester U.P. 1968.
MES :: *Medieval English Songs.* Ed. E.J. Dobson and F.Ll. Harrison. London: Faber and Faber.1979.

OTHER REFERENCES

Bennett, J.A.W. (ed.) (1955). *Devotional Pieces in Verse and Prose.* Scottish Text Society. Edinburgh and London.
Dronke, P. (1978). *The Medieval Lyric.* 2nd ed. London: Hutchinson.
Gray, D. (1972). *Themes and Images in the Medieval English Religious Lyric.* London: Routledge and Kegan Paul.
Greene, R.L. (1977). *The Early English Carols.* 2nd ed. Oxford: O.U.P.
Kinsley, J. (ed.) (1979). *The Poems of William Dunbar.* Oxford: O.U.P.
Pearsall, D. (1977). *Old and Middle English Poetry.* London: Routledge and Kegan Paul.
Sitwell, E. (1972). *A Poet's Notebook.* Westport, CT: Greenwood (1st publ. London: Macmillan 1943).
Wenzel, S. (1978). *Verses in Sermons.* Cambridge, MA: Harvard U.P.
Wilson, E. (ed.) (1973). *A Descriptive Index of the English Lyrics in John of Grimestone's Preaching Book.* Medium Ævum Monographs, N.S. II. Oxford.
Woolf, R. (1968). *The English Religious Lyric in the Middle Ages.* Oxford: O.U.P.

ST KENELM AND THE LEGENDS OF THE ENGLISH SAINTS IN THE *SOUTH ENGLISH LEGENDARY*

RENEE HAMELINCK
(Utrecht)

When the *South English Legendary* (*SEL*) was composed in the Worcester area at the end of the thirteenth century, collections of saints' legends existed in various countries and in different languages. They were based on a collection of saints' legends in Latin, the *Legenda Aurea*. However, "national saints tended to become appended to or inserted into *LgA* [*Legenda Aurea*] manuscripts in different European countries" (Görlach, 1973:23). Almost a fifth of the legends assembled in the *SEL* are about English saints. Because of the compiler's decision to order the legends according to the distribution of the saints' feastdays over the year, the legends about the English saints are scattered over the entire work. As a result, the underlying unity of the legends does not immediately become clear, but a closer examination of the material reveals that the compiler has apparently selected the legends to serve specific purposes.

Together the legends relate the history of the English church from the time when Christianity was first brought to England by St Augustine up to the thirteenth century when the *SEL* was composed. The most recently canonized saint in the collection is Edmund Rich, Archbishop of Canterbury, whose canonization took place some fifty years before the collection was compiled. The development of the English church as related in the legends shows how, after a period of prosperity under the Anglo-Saxon kings, its position becomes increasingly weakened after the Norman kings came to power. When St Augustine is sent to England on a mission to convert the people, he expects a hostile reception. Contrary to his expectations, the heathen King Ethelbert, although not willing to accept the new religion before thoroughly examining it, receives the missionary well and gives him ample freedom to carry out his preaching activities. When he has come to the conclusion that the new religion is a good one, he full-heartedly accepts it. Thus a period of prosperity for the Christian church under the Anglo-Saxon kings commences. The kings

support the church and encourage its bishops in the spreading of the
new faith throughout the country.

The relationship between the kings and the church is one of the
main points of interest in the legends about the English saints. Some
of the Anglo-Saxon kings take the church's welfare so much to heart
that they themselves become saints, as is the case with the kings
Oswald, Edward the Elder and Edward the Confessor. When the
king and the church support each other, prosperity comes to the
people of the country. This can be seen in the legend of St Edward
the Elder, who relies heavily upon the advice of his bishop Dunstan,
who

> ... was glad of him . and al is lond also
> Of such king þat was hore louerd . þat fonde so wel to do
> God pais þer was in Engelond . & loue & ioye inou
> Richesse and al oþer god . for elles it were wou
> For wanne þe heued haþ Godes grace . & loueþ alle gode
> Wonder hit were bote al his . þe betere bistode
>   *Edward the Elder*, 23-8[1]

> (... was pleased with him, and so was his whole country with such
> a king as their lord was, who tried to do so well. There was great
> peace in England, and plenty of love and joy, wealth and all other
> goods, because otherwise it would be a sad truth. For when the
> head has God's grace, and loves all goodness, it would be strange if
> all his [people] did not prosper the better.)

The prosperity of England depends directly upon the king, who can
make his country prosper by listening to the advice of his ecclesiastical counsellors, and thus deserve God's grace. When the king acts
against God's wish, it is not only the church, but the entire country
which suffers as a result. When King Ethelred comes to the throne
after murdering his stepbrother King Edward, Bishop Dunstan pre-
dicts great misery which will not only affect the king but also

> ... þe lond folk of Engelond . þat no gult nabbeþ þerto
> For more wrechede & sorwe . þer comeþ bi þine daye
> Into Engelond uor þulke sunne . þan me euere iseye
>   *Edward the Elder*, 110-12

---

[1] All quotations are from the text edition by D'Evelyn and Mill (1956-9).

(... the people of England, who have no guilt in it. For greater
misery and sorrow will come in your time to England because of
that sin, than has ever been seen.)

It is not until Ethelred's son, Edward the Confessor, becomes king
that England prospers again.

In the legends about the English saints, the early English
period is looked back upon with nostalgia. The time when the head
of state and the church are supporting each other comes to an end
with the death of the last Anglo-Saxon king, Edward the Confessor.
The tragedy which affects the country is described in the legend of St
Wulfstan.

> Four ȝer he [Wulfstan] hadde bissop ibe[o] . & noȝt
> follich fyue
> To seint Edward þe holy king . wende out of þis liue
> To gret ruþe to al Engelonde . so weilawei þe stonde
> For strange men þer come suþþe . & broȝte Engelond
> to gronde
> *Wulfstan, 57-60*

(He had been bishop for four years, and not fully five, when St
Edward, the holy king, departed from this life, which was a cause
of great sorrow to all England, alas the time! For foreign men came
afterwards, and brought England to ruin.)

The decline of the English church starts with the arrival of
William the Conqueror, who brought England under Norman and
feudal rule. From then on the legends of the English saints no longer
describe a state of harmony between the ruler and the church, but the
saints meet growing opposition in their plans and actions for the
benefit of the church. While the earlier legends show that, in general, the Anglo-Saxon kings were more than willing to listen to their
bishops' advice, the Norman kings, for their part, were not, resent-
ing the bishops' opinions where these differed from their own, and
fearing encroachment upon the power of the king. But the conflict is
not only one between secular ruler and saint: it is a conflict between
old values and new, which were forced upon the English by the
invaders. The foreign rulers are definitely not accepted as the
rightful kings of England, as is stated in unambiguous terms in the
legend of St Wulfstan in the Ashmole MS. The battle between Harold
and William the Conqueror brings the Norman king victory and
Harold

... was byneþe ibroʒt . & ouercome attelaste
& ibroʒt to gronde & alle his . & al engelond also
Ibrouʒt in strange menne hond . þat lute riʒt hadde

þerto
Þat neuer eft hit ne com aʒen . to riʒt heires non
Vnkunde heires ʒut hi beþ . oure kynges euerichon
Wulfstan, 86-90

(... was brought down, and was overcome at last, and he and all his
men perished, and also all of England was brought into strange
men's hands, who had little right to it. So that it was never afterwards restored to any rightful heir. They are still unrightful heirs,
each one of our kings.)

The crisis between worldly ruler and saint reaches its climax
in the conflict between Archbishop Thomas Becket and King Henry
II. Due to the compiler's decision to order the legends according to
the distribution of the saints' feastdays over the year, the legend of
Thomas Becket, whose festival was on 29th December, is the last one
of the collection, and was clearly intended to be its highlight. The
conflicts between the archbishop and the king over the rights of the
church are described in great detail. Whereas the king wants Becket's
complete submission to his wishes, the archbishop thinks that Henry
is trying to curtail the power of the church and he is only willing to
obey the king's commands when they do not endanger the church's
power. As the tension between the two men mounts, the only solution
to the problem seems to be Becket's death. To defend the church's
rights the saint is willing to suffer martyrdom:

Icham for Holy Churche riʒte . iredy þane deþ auonge
Biddeþ for me for Godes loue . and for Holy Churche

also
Þat geþ almest nou to gronde . bote God nyme ʒeme

þertwo
Thomas Becket, 1982-4

(I am ready then to receive death for the right of the Holy Church.
Pray for me for God's love and also for the Holy Church which is
now almost destroyed, unless God takes heed of it.)

When Henry's knights murder Becket on the consecrated ground of
Canterbury Cathedral, the tragic climax in the history of the English
church has been reached. A choice has been made in favour of secular power and against the church.

But Becket is more than a representative of the church: his opposition to the unjust plans of the king and his stubbornness in defending his rights symbolize a growing self-awareness among the English people who are becoming increasingly discontented with the foreign rulers and desire to have the good times under the Anglo-Saxon kings restored.

Among the legends about the English saints in the *SEL* the legend of St Kenelm takes up an interesting position. The legend relates how Kenelm succeeds his father to the throne of Mercia when he is only seven years old. His sister Quendride resents his power and plans to have her brother murdered. It is Kenelm's guardian Askebert who performs the foul act by decapitating the boy and hiding his body in the forest. When people have forgotten about Kenelm, a cow makes it its habit to sleep on the spot where the king is buried. Although the animal's behaviour is believed to have a miraculous meaning, this is not understood until God reveals in a message from Heaven to the Pope in Rome the place where Kenelm's body lies hidden. Soon the body is discovered, and the young king is buried beside his father in Winchcombe, whereas Quendride receives her just punishment when she is dragged out of town and her body is thrown into a ditch.

Although Kenelm is venerated as a martyr in the *SEL*, he did not suffer death because of his faith, and therefore cannot strictly be called a martyr. His case is not unique: the *SEL* also includes King Edward in its list of martyrs, although this king was murdered over a matter of succession to the throne, and not as a result of his religious opinions. The events described in Edward's legend correspond with the historical facts, whereas there is no doubt that the story of Kenelm's life and death does not correspond with what is known about him. According to the most important historical document of the Anglo-Saxon period, *the Anglo-Saxon Chronicle*, Kenelm's father, King Kenulf, was succeeded by his brother Cedwulf. Kenelm is not mentioned at all in the *Chronicle*, and the only historical evidence which exists of him is a number of documents which he signed as "Cynhelm princeps" or "Cynhelm dux" between 803 and 811, when he must have been about fourteen years old. This means that Kenelm was at least twenty-four when his father died in 819, and not a boy of seven as is stated in the legend.[2] Little historical

---

[2] For a more detailed description of the historical facts about Kenelm, see Von Antropoff, 1956:23-5.

value can be attached to the description of Quendride, Kenelm's wicked sister, either. As it is known that she was an abbess during her lifetime, there seems to be no reason to assume that she had wanted to murder her brother. It is therefore likely that the characters of the two leading persons in the legend, Kenelm and Quendride, were adapted to suit their roles: a child who is martyred is more pathetic than an adult, and Quendride has to oppose this child with full wickedness so that his virtue is demonstrated more clearly.

One of the reasons justifying the inclusion of Kenelm's legend in the *SEL* is the saint's immense popularity in the south of England, where the *SEL* was compiled. It is even likely that people had begun to worship Kenelm as a saint long before he was officially canonized. Quite frequently a saint was canonized under pressure of the popularity he enjoyed among the common people (De Grijs, 1983:18). The centre of Kenelm's veneration was in Winchcombe, and it was there that many people assembled on his feastday on 17th July. In his *De Gestis Regum Anglorum* William of Malmesbury claims that nowhere in England did so many people gather as on Kenelm's Feastday, although it must be admitted that a large crowd might also have been attracted by the big annual market which was held in Winchcombe on the same day (see Von Antropoff, 1956:29-30). There is no doubt, however, that Kenelm was a particularly popular saint among the common people, and it is especially at this audience that the legend of the saint in the *SEL* is directed.

The second reason why Kenelm's legend was included in the collection is that it fits in with the sentiments expressed in the group of legends about the English saints, as will become evident when the legend is discussed in more detail.

The story opens with a long description of Anglo-Saxon England at the time of Kenelm. It describes the state of England before the invasions, the 'pure kingdom'. The purpose of the long description, which takes up about one-sixth of the total length of the legend, is twofold. Firstly it is meant to demonstrate that Mercia was the most powerful of the five kingdoms, which explains why Kenelm's sister is envious of her brother's wealth when he becomes king. It is Quendride's envy which causes Kenelm's tragic death and triggers off the action in the narrative. The description is also meant to remind the audience of the history of the country—a history they could be proud of. The undertone of nationalistic pride accords with that found in the other legends of English saints and fits in with the policy of King Edward I, who made a conscious effort to emphasize his Anglo-Saxon roots. Named after the last great Anglo-Saxon king, Edward the Confessor, Edward I suppressed his Norman descent and sought to strengthen his grip on the English throne by stressing his Anglo-Saxon lineage, and by stimulating a new nationalistic feeling in his subjects.

Whereas the description of the Anglo-Saxon kingdoms was based on historical truth, the description of Kenelm and Quendride was not, as has been suggested above. All through the legend Kenelm's youth is emphasized, and it is shown how an innocent child falls victim to the wicked intentions of the adults surrounding him. Kenelm's innocence causes God's grace to rest upon him. When the child is not affected by the poison which Quendride administers to him in her first attempt to dispose of her brother, it is explained to the audience that God will not allow Kenelm to be martyred so easily. It becomes clear that the child has to fulfil a special role in the Divine Plan. There is no indication that Kenelm himself is aware of his special position in God's plan—he remains ignorant of the harm which his sister tried to conflict upon him.

In many legends God's working a miracle for the saint creates an emotional distance between the saint and the audience. The saint no longer moves on the same level as other people: he has transcended that and has grown in spiritual posture. This alienation has consciously been avoided in *St Kenelm* by emphasizing the saint's ignorance of God's design and by the fact that he is only a child. The frequent repetition of the word "child" serves to keep Kenelm on a level with the audience, who remain emotionally involved with him.

The same innocence speaks from Kenelm's inability to interpret the dream he has about the ash-tree. He dreams how his dearest friend cuts down the tree with the intention of killing Kenelm who was sitting on one of its boughs. When the tree falls, Kenelm changes into a white dove and flies to Heaven. From a narrative point of view, the recounting of the dream heightens the suspense in the story: as Kenelm's nurse explains to the boy, the dream foreshadows his death. But the dream is also symbolic of God's grace resting upon the young king: the white dove which flies to Heaven symbolizes Kenelm's soul which will be taken up into the glory of Heaven. The dove is also a symbol of hope. Although Kenelm may be overcome by evil when his guardian murders him, his death will not remain unavenged, and is indeed necessary to reveal God's power, which is the people's hope.

When the people have forgotten about Kenelm after he has
been murdered, it is *a dombe best wiþoute witte* (1.220: 'a dumb
animal without intelligence') which is chosen as the instrument for
God's miracle. The cow always returns to the spot where the king's
body lies hidden. It does not eat, but still produces more milk every
day, which makes the composer exclaim:

> Wo so hadde such kun inowe . he nere noʒt bymene
> Þei is larder were nei do . and is somer lese lene
> *St Kenelm* 235-6

> (Who possessed enough of such cows need not be pitied, even if his
> provision chamber were almost empty, and his summer pasture
> lean.)

This observation, which might well have been a later addition to the
text by the scribe, clearly wants to evoke a direct response from the
audience, who, judging from the nature of the remark, cannot have
been an upper class one. Most of the legends in the *SEL* aim at a
lower class audience; it is mainly for them that the saints work their
miracles.

The miracle of the cow also leads to another miracle, for although the common people recognize the cow's behaviour as miraculous, they cannot fully interpret its meaning. Although God's miracles can be seen by all men, the church is needed to explain them for
them. In the legend of Kenelm, it is God Himself who explains the
miracle to His people. This happens when God sends a *writ* from
Heaven to the Pope in Rome, which states:

> In Clent Coubach Kenelm kinges bern
> Liþ vnder a þorn heued bireued
> *St Kenelm* 267-8

> (In Cowbach in Clent lies Kenelm, the king's son, under a thorn-
> tree, deprived of his head.)

The message provides the information necessary to understand the
cow's behaviour. This miracle is the highlight of the legend, and it
explains why *St Kenelm* takes up a key position among the legends of
the English saints in the *SEL*. The letter with God's explanation
comes straight from Heaven and is directed to the English people,
which is made clear by the fact that it is written in English. The Pope
cannot understand the divine message, but the English people can!

Kenelm's martyrdom, then, was necessary for God to reveal the special place which the English have in His divine plan. It is no wonder that this writing is stated to be the most wonderful relic: *Wat noblore relike miȝte be[o] . i necan noȝt vnderstonde* (1.274: 'I cannot perceive what more splendid relic there could be').

The miracle links the different layers of the narrative. In the story proper it leads to the discovery of the body and the restoring of justice. When Kenelm's body is carried back to the town of Winchcombe, Quendride loses her power to inflict harm upon others. When she tries to curse her brother's corpse, the curse falls upon herself and her eyes fall out. Thus she is punished for her misdeeds. Balance is restored when she is dragged out of town and thrown into a ditch and dies a shameful death, whereas Kenelm's remains are carried into Winchcombe in triumph and are enshrined in the abbey.

The miracle also demonstrates that God uses His saints as an instrument to reveal His love for the people. The virtuous Anglo-Saxon boy-king Kenelm is proof of this. Hence the legend of Kenelm takes the audience back to the good Anglo-Saxon times when God's love was expressed so openly, and for everyone to see. The *SEL* regrets that those times were over with the coming of the Norman rulers, whose desire for absolute power inflicts harm upon the church and makes it difficult for the people to discover God's intentions. All that is left of the miracles worked for the English people in the old times are the saints' relics and the places where the miracles were worked for the saints. Such a place is the well which springs to quench the thirst of the people who are carrying Kenelm's body back from the forest to Winchcombe. The well still existed when the legend was composed, and it is said that

> Wel faire it is iheled nou . wiþ freo ston as riȝt is
> Iredi ech mon to drinke of . þat comeþ þeruorþ iwis
> Þe monkes suþþe of Winchecombe . irered habbeþ þere
>   biside
> A uair chapel of sein Kenelm . þat men secheþ wyde
> *St Kenelm* 333-6

(Now it is beautifully covered, with a slab of limestone as it should be. May every person who comes to this place be prepared to drink from it. Afterwards the monks of Winchcombe erected beside it a beautiful chapel of St Kenelm, which people come to visit from afar.)

Places like Winchcombe were the tangible evidence of God's power and His love for the English people.

Although at first sight the legend of St Kenelm seems little more than a fairytale-like story about a boy saint, the legend acquires a deeper meaning when seen in the light of the legends about the English saints as a group in the *South English Legendary*. Perhaps more strongly than in any of the other legends, it expresses the longing for the old Anglo-Saxon times when God's grace so openly rested upon England and its inhabitants. Since the coming of the Norman kings who acted against the benefit of the church, this grace is no more to be seen. Or, to quote the words of Bishop Dunstan once more, it is *þe lond folk of Engelond . þat no gult nabbeþ þerto* who suffer most.

REFERENCES

De Grijs, F.J.A. (1983). Heiligen, wat zijn dat eigenlijk? In: R.E.V. Stuip and C. Vellekoop (eds.). *Andere Structuren, Andere Heiligen*. Utrecht: HES. 13-32.
D'Evelyn, C., and A.J. Mill (eds.) (1956-59). *The South English Legendary*. 3 Vols. EETS, OS 235, 236, 244.
Görlach, M. (1973). *The Textual Tradition of the South English Legendary*. Leeds Texts and Monographs, New Series 6. Leeds.
Von Antropoff, R. (1965). *Die Entwicklung der Kenelm Legende*. Dissertation. Bonn.

HAVELOK THE DANE
A NON-COURTLY ROMANCE

HENK AERTSEN
(Vrije Universiteit, Amsterdam)

As Bennett points out (1986:121), the term 'romance' was first applied to classical and pseudo-classical narratives written in the vernacular language of France, such as the *Roman d'Enéas* and the *Roman de Thebes,* to distinguish them from their Latin originals. Thus a *roman* is a story in Latin on a classical subject that was *romanicé* or 'romanced', i.e. translated into French, and the word *roman* can therefore be rendered into Modern English simply as 'the French book' (cf. Everett, 1955:2).[1] At a later stage, the term 'romance', just like the OF *roman*, came to be used for "those tales of knights and their doings for which the French were first famous, without regard to the language in which they were written" (Everett, 1955:3).

A term related to 'romance' is *gest(e)*, which Bennett calls "a subspecimen of romance", indicating, he says, "that some historical truth is claimed for the narrative" (1986:121). The Middle English word *gest(e)*, usually rendered as 'narrative, story', is a borrowing from Old French and is ultimately derived from Latin *gesta* 'deeds, exploits; events'.

The terms 'romance' and 'geste' both occur in the romance under discussion, *Havelok the Dane* [2] (henceforth *HD*). They are found almost side by side in the catalogue of royal entertainments which

---

[1] A fuller derivation and explanation of the word *romance* is given by Baugh (1948:173, note 1):

> The word *romance* comes from a Latin adverb *romanice*, meaning "in the Roman manner" (*loqui romanice*, to speak in the Roman manner, i.e. speak colloquial Latin). In time, with the change of Vulgar Latin into the various romance languages, it came to mean more particularly French, and then something written in French, especially something translated from Latin.

[2] All quotations from *HD* have been taken from the edition by Skeat as revised by Sisam (Skeat and Sisam, 1915). The poem has also been edited by Holthausen (1928), and by French and Hale (1964:71-176) and Schmidt and Jacobs (1980: i.37-121) for their anthologies, while annotated selections have appeared in most Middle English readers. A new authoritative, but rather expensive, edition by Smithers has recently been published (1987).

were part of the festivities following Havelok's coronation as king of
Denmark:

> Hwan he was king, þer mouhte men se
> Þe moste ioie þat mouhte be: ...
> Romanz-reding on þe bok;
> Þer mouhte men here þe geste singe,
> Þe gleumen on þe tabour dinge.   (2320-21, 2327-9)

(When he was king, one could see there the greatest gaiety that
could be: ... reading of romances in the book; there one could hear
the stories being sung, and the minstrels beating the drum.)

We see that the poet speaks of 'reading of romances' and of 'singing
of *gestes*', and this distinction is commented on by Schmidt and
Jacobs in the following way (1980:i.184):

> The contrast seems to be one between works *read* out
> aloud (courtly 'romances' in French) and works *sung*,
> perhaps by the gleemen who strike the tabor ('gestes' in
> the language of the ordinary people). The *Havelok*-poet
> has called his own work a 'gest' (2989[3]) not a 'romanz'
> (which is probably what he would have called his
> French source, if he had one), but he can hardly have
> intended it to be 'sung'.

This interpretation of *gestes* does not seem to be consistent with their
rendering of this word in the gloss at the foot of p.102, which reads
"*gestes*, epics ('chansons de geste')", because what they say about the
Havelok poet calling his own work a 'gest' is equally true of epics:
epics can hardly have been intended to be sung either. French and
Hale divide lines 2327-9 differently: whereas Schmidt and Jacobs
link the singing of *gestes* to the minstrels or gleemen of the next line,
French and Hale take the first two lines together and have no part
for the drum-beating minstrels in the reading of romances or the
singing of *gestes*, since their note to these lines reads (1964:152):
"Note that some of the gestes here were sung; the readers and singers
were the aristocrats among minstrels, and trick drummers were not

---

[3] The line-numbering in Schmidt and Jacobs' edition of *HD* differs from that in the
edition from which we quote, the Skeat-Sisam edition.

their equals." In additon to the contrast between works to be read out and works to be sung, these notes by Schmidt and Jacobs and by French and Hale establish another contrast, although they do so less explicitly—it is a contrast between upper and lower-class audiences, i.e. the people of the court and the ordinary people. As Schmidt and Jacobs say in the note quoted above, "the *Havelok*-poet has called his own work a 'gest'", when he addresses his audience at the end of the poem in a kind of epilogue: *Nu haue ye herd þe gest al þoru / Of Hauelok and of Goldeborw* (ll.2984-5: 'Now you have heard the story of Havelok and Goldeboru completely, from beginning to end').

   That the term 'gest' may also denote romances written for the lower classes, or for non-courtly audiences, is supported by *HD* and by the way in which it presents its subject-matter: Staines, for instance, says that the poet "addressed himself to a particular audience: the lower classes" (1976:612). The same idea had been expressed by others before Staines: Creek was one of the first to recognize the "homely and popular elements" in *HD*, but his conclusion that the poem "was intended not for the hall, but for the inn or street" (1915: 210) is unfortunately based on the prologue and epilogue, which may be minstrel additions; yet he points out a great many homely details in other parts of the poem, as well as some homely figures of speech and proverbial expressions of "the folk", which suggest that "the English redactor was one with an intimate and sympathetic acquaintance with humble life" (1915: 207). *HD*, Creek says (1915:203), "seems to introduce us to the atmosphere of humble life of medieval England. There is no other English romance which does this to an equal extent, and there are scarcely any which do so at all." In other words, *HD* is at least in this respect unique, and this is also noted by Pearsall (1965:98):

> *Havelok* is unique among English romances in its systematic realisation of the story in terms of humble everyday life. (...) Havelok's qualities—his instinct for survival, opportunism, modesty, industry, lack of sentiment, practical good sense, love of children—are the virtues of common people. (...) *Havelok* has a claim, if any English romance has, to be regarded as the genuine expression of popular consciousness.

Hanning (1967:605) comes to a similar evaluation: "The meaning itself ... is no less impressive for being presented in a popular rather than a courtly garb." Mehl's conclusion (1968:166) is that "There is no doubt that the poem is addressed not to a courtly, but to a middle-class audience, with the intention of appealing to a great variety of tastes."

Audience and subject-matter thus explain Schmidt and Jacobs' characterization of *HD* as "a 'non-courtly' poem" (1980:i.8), but this should come as no surprise, since Pearsall (1965:91) has shown that

> the social context of Middle English romance ... is overwhelmingly popular and non-courtly. True courtly romance had no real vogue in English, since the audience which could appreciate it, at the time when it was fashionable, was French-speaking. The only exceptions are the alliterative romances and the late adaptations of the genre by Chaucer. The audience of Middle English romances is primarily a lower or lower-middle class audience.

The poet also uses other terms with reference to the poem. In the prologue and epilogue he calls it a *rym* (ll.21, 23, 2995, 2998), meaning "a riming poem, song, or ballad; a verse narrative" according to the *MED*. The Prologue also has the term *tale* (ll.3, 5 12), which is specifically used for narratives delivered orally. A similar term is *spelle*, which occurs in l.338: *Say we nou forth in ure spelle!* ('Let us now proceed with the telling of our story!') The function of this line is to mark the transition between the two introductory episodes of the poem, one being set in England and dealing with the death of King Athelwold and the appointment of Earl Godrich as the guardian of Athelwold's infant daughter Goldeboru, the other describing similar events and a similar state of affairs in Denmark, the death of King Birkabeyn and the appointment of Earl Godard as the guardian of Birkabeyn's infant children Swanborough, Elfled and Havelok. Yet in spite of the specific function of this line in the poem, there is no special meaning in the use of the word *spelle*, which is simply a term that was "commonly used throughout the mediaeval period in England to refer to speech and oral accounts in general" (Strohm, 1971:353).

Of the two terms *spelle* and *tale*, the latter was the more general, according to Strohm, and was used even when the narrative could be defined more narrowly as a *storie* (used in ll.1641 and 1734), *tretys*, or *lyf* (i.e. saint's life, see below). *Spelle*, Strohm says, was "somewhat more restricted in range, usually to oral narratives with limited scope and immediate impact" (1971:353). Both these qualifications may apply to the use of *spelle* in l.338: the introductory episodes are of limited scope in that they set the scene and provide the background for the subsequent development of the plot, but they also have an immediate impact in that they make the audience side with the hero against his adversaries, the narrator acting as an intermediary in this respect (cf. Mehl, 1968:26, 167).

The title of Skeat's edition, *The Lay of Havelok the Dane*, suggests that Skeat considered the poem to be "an English equivalent to the Anglo-Norman *Lai d'Haveloc*" (Bennett, 1986:154). It is true that the Anglo-Norman poem is called a *lai* in its opening lines, but this is only a trick, as Bennett explains, because the poet is "trying, like Chaucer with his *Franklin's Tale* much later, to pass off his poem as a Breton lay though in fact he based it on a known literary work, Gaimar's *Histoire des Engleis*" (1986:154-5). What is perhaps more important in this respect is that the Middle English poem is too different from the Anglo-Norman *Lai* to be considered an English equivalent to it. The Anglo-Norman poem is an upper-class or courtly romance, dealing with *noble fez* ('noble feats') and *l'aventure d'un riche rei / E de plusurs altres baruns* ('the adventure of a great king and of several other barons'), whereas in *HD* there is "the atmosphere of humble life of medieval England" (Creek, 1915:203). This difference is illustrated, for instance, by Grim, who is one of the barons in the Anglo-Norman *Lai*, but he is merely a fisherman in *HD*. The conclusion, therefore, can only be that the title of Skeat's edition is somewhat unfortunate.

In the manuscript the poem appears with the heading

> Incipit Vita Hauelok quondam Rex Anglie et Denemarchie
>
> (Here begins the Life of Havelok, formerly King of England and Denmark)

The term *vita* was the usual name for the genre known as the 'saint's life', and its application to the Havelok story gives rise to a number

of interesting observations[4], of a speculative nature it is true, since it
cannot be ascertained whether the Latin title is authentic (i.e. given
by the poet) or whether it is the invention of the scribe who copied
the manuscript. It is not altogether unusual for a romance to be
entitled 'The Life of ...', as *Ipomadon B*, for instance, has this title,
but the term *vita* has religious associations, which would suggest, if
the title is the author's, that he was a cleric. This view would support
Creek's conclusion (1915:211) that "the author belonged to the
clergy", a conclusion he reached on the basis of "the emphasis [in the
poem] on religious matters, the insistence on the moral aspects of the
story, the love of proverbial wisdom" and especially because of "two
scraps of Latin" in the poem, both of which are "of a religious
character": *Benedicamus domino* (1.20: 'Let us bless the Lord') and
"In manus tuas," loude he seyde (1.228: '"Into your hands," he said
loudly').

   HD is followed by *King Horn* in MS Laud Misc. 108, where
these two romances are preceded and followed by a number of
saints' lives: the scribe may have felt that these two poems would not
be out of place in a collection of saints' lives. Schmidt and Jacobs
(1980:i.7) define the saint's life by its twofold purpose:

> to praise God by showing His marvellous works in the
> lives of chosen individuals, and to assure the audience
> that God's omnipresence often took the specific form of
> intervention in the lives of men, now loving, now
> vengeful.

These two aspects of a saint's life are both present in *HD*: "to praise
God" is exactly what the poet (or scribe or minstrel) calls on his
audience to do (1.20, quoted above), and Havelok may be regarded as
"a divinely favoured individual in whose life God intervenes not on
one but on several occasions" (Schmidt and Jacobs, 1980:i.7). This
seems to link up well with the way in which Staines (1976:613)
characterizes the poem:

> It is first and foremost an idealized biography cast in the
> form of a tale of action. The biography concentrates,

[4] For some of these observations I am indebted to Schmidt and Jacobs (1980:i.7,
173). Their explanation of the implications of the term *vita* has been supplemented
by me with the references to Creek, Staines, Mehl and *HD*, 1.12.

not on the most exciting moments of Havelok's life, but
rather on those episodes which delineate most clearly
the poet's conception of the ideal king.

The ideal king is the good king, the king who "works for the welfare
of his subjects, [who] is the protector of the poor, the orphaned, and
the widowed, [who] is the provider of the lower classes, [who] must
be a God-fearing individual, since the beginning of wisdom is fear of
the Lord" (Staines, 1976:614[5]). Note how well this description of the
good king fits the portrait of King Athelwold in *HD* (ll.27-105): the
orphaned and the widowed are explicitly mentioned (ll.75, 79), and
Athelwold *louede god with al his miht, And holi kirke, and soth, and
riht* (ll.35-6: 'loved God with all his might, and the Holy Church,
and truth and justice'). Athelwold, in other words, is the perfect
Christian king, and at the end of the poem it is Havelok who is the
right king in power (cf. Weiss, 1969:249-50). The poem shows, as it
were, how Havelok develops these innate qualities of the good and
perfect king, and it is precisely these qualities that are emphasized in
saints' lives.[6]

Mehl (1968:172) mentions another feature that *HD* shares with
some of the saints' lives:

the poem ... resembles the *vitae* of some saints in that it
presents models of human behaviour and provides
instruction as well as entertainment, in a more specific
sense than can be said of the shorter romances. There is
no 'escapism' in this poem.

"It ... provides instruction": this is in fact what the Prologue says the
poem does: *And þe tale ye mowen y-lere* (l.12: 'And you can learn
from the story'). However, it is also with respect to another important distinction between *vitae* or saints' lives and romances that *HD*
seems more to resemble a *vita* than a romance: saints' lives describe
historical persons (though their biographies may contain non-his-

5 Staines here paraphrases the description of the ideal king in John of Salisbury's
Policraticus, a mid-twelfth-century political treatise, which may well have been the
model for the political ideas underlying *HD*. Staines quotes and translates in
footnotes the passages from the *Policraticus* which he paraphrases.
6 Cf. Renée Hamelinck's study on "St Kenelm and the *South-English Legendary*"
in this volume.

torical details), whereas romances do not, since they or most of them create a character and assign a given ideal to this fictitious character. Saints' lives and romances are therefore different in their respective starting-points: a saint's life starts from a historical person with an idealized quality, while a romance starts from an ideal and creates a fictitious character to represent this ideal. In the case of *HD*, the ideal is that of the good king (cf. the quote from Staines above), and the historicity of the character of Havelok has been the subject of a long debate, which is summarized in the Skeat-Sisam edition of *HD* (pp.xxv-vi): the name *Havelok* may be a form of the Celtic name *Abloc* or *Abloec*, an adaptation of ON *Olaf-r*, OE *Anlaf*, in which case the name may refer to the "famous Viking, Olaf Sictricson, who was on the defeated side at Brunanburh in 937", but the section just referred to in the Introduction to the Skeat-Sisam edition also mentions other potential candidates. The difference between a saint's life and a romance can be summed up in this way: the *vita* tells a story from the point of view of the person, the romance from that of the ideal, or, in the *vita* it is the person who speaks, in romance it is the ideal.

Schmidt and Jacobs (1980:i.1) give a rather simple definition of the subject-matter of Middle English romances: "The medieval English romances are stories in verse which deal with the adventures of noble men and women and which end happily." They admit that this definition is vague, but it is good enough in view of the evidence. It is possible, they maintain, to establish certain prominent features as universal and defining features of the genre: 'fighting' or 'the marvellous' are common in romances, but by no means universal, as there is no fighting in *Floris and Blauncheflour* and *Athelston*, and 'the marvellous' is lacking in *Ipomadon*. Love is not a defining feature either: it "plays an important part in French but a smaller part in English romance"; nor is the 'courtly' tone such a feature: it is "found in the best single English romance, *Sir Gawain and the Green Knight*, but not in *Havelok*, which is arguably the second best" (1980:i.1).

Bennett (1986:122) has a similar general definition of the subject-matter of romances, and immediately adds that the romance under discussion, *HD*, does not conform to this description in two respects:

> Most romances, ..., narrate the adventures of some hero
> of chivalry. Yet the eponymous hero of *Havelok*, though
> of royal birth, can hardly be called such a hero. What
> such a tale has in common with the French romances
> from which so many English romances derive is the ele-
> ment of perilous adventure and feats of martial prowess.
> Love, which later ages were to associate with romance,
> plays a very minor part in *Havelok*.

There are, then, three respects in which *HD* stands out from the
other Middle English romances: its lack of a 'courtly' tone (cf.
Creek's observation, quoted above, that there is in *HD* "the atmosphere of humble life in medieval England" [1915:203]), the absence
of a noble hero, and the absence of love. On the other hand, it cannot
be denied that Havelok *is* the hero and that his deeds are dealt with in
the romance. That is why Mehl's description (1968:17) of the subject-matter of the Middle English romances—"Most of the Middle
English romances are devoted to the glorification of some particular
hero. This is not true of the French romances to the same extent."—
is especially relevant to *HD*: Mehl refrains from speaking of a hero
of chivalry, he simply says "hero", nor does he mention love as an
important feature of romances.

There are various classifications of Middle English romances. The
traditional classification is the one according to the cycles of stories
on which the romances are based. It ultimately goes back to a passage in one of the poems of the late-twelfth-century French poet Jean
Bodel, in which he speaks of *trois matières* ('three matters'), *de
France et de Bretaigne et de Rome la grant* ('of France and of
Britain and of Rome the great').[7] This division must have been
unsatisfactory from the start, even if only applied to Bodel's own
time and to the literature of his day, because it "very imperfectly
sums up the riches and the variety of French romantic themes" and
especially because "the 'matter of Rome' includes the whole of antiquity, the tales of Thebes and Troy, the wars of Alexander" (Ker,

---

[7] This passage has been quoted, among others, by Schofield (1906:145), by Baugh
(1948:174), and also by Ker (1907:279, note 2):
    Ne sont que trois matières à nul home attendant,
    De France et de Bretaigne et de Rome la grant.
                  Jean Bodel, *Chanson de Saisnes*.

1907:279). Wilson (1968:199) comments on the inadequacy of
Bodel's division for the development of the genre during the following 200 years, when "a great number of new romance themes were
introduced, mainly from the east... [which] are usually somewhat
negligently grouped together as 'Miscellaneous Romances'. (...) In
addition there grew up in England a class of romance peculiar to the
country and based, though often very remotely, on the earlier
history of England. In imitation of Bodel's classification these are
usually grouped together under the title of the 'Matter of England'."
In this classification according to narrative material *HD* obviously
belongs to the 'Matter of England', even though the hero is a Dane,
but one "whose fortunes are tied up with England and whose prin-
cipal adventures take place on the island" (Baugh, 1948:175); we
may add that the hero even rose to be king of England.

Mehl (1968:31-2) rejects the classification according to 'matters' on two grounds. Like Wilson, he feels that the term 'Miscellaneous Romances' does not do full justice to the romances that come
under this heading only because they "have not necessarily anything
in common beyond the fact that they cannot be fitted into any of the
matières." His second reason for rejecting this kind of classification
is of a more general nature: "in most cases there is no logical and
unambiguous correspondence between material and form, between a
certain story and a poem based on it." This seems to echo Pearsall's
observation that whereas stories are the property of everyone, "a
formal tradition is the property only of its practitioners, and it is
through its formal and stylistic aspects ... that the history of romance can be most objectively analysed" (1965: 96). In this analysis
Pearsall distinguishes between romances written in four-stress
couplets and those in tail-rhyme, and this distinction, he says, "is a
very real one, for it corresponds to a more fundamental division
between 'epic romance' and 'lyric romance', the former more
prosaic, realistic, historical and martial, the latter more emotive,
more concerned with love, faith, constancy and the marvellous." In
Pearsall's classification *HD* is grouped among the 'epic romances',
even though "the marvellous" can be said to be represented in the
poem in Havelok's so-called birth-marks (see below).

Mehl calls Pearsall's distinction between epic romance and
lyric romance "somewhat questionable" (1968:269, note 21), and
proposes a classification which is based on length and which distinguishes between 'shorter' and 'longer' works. He admits that this
distinction may appear somewhat oversimplified but explains that

"size is by no means an external feature. It conditions the treatment of the story, the dramatic movement and the narrative structure" (1968:36). He links the question of size to the practice of oral delivery. There appears to be a large group of poems of between five and twelve hundred lines, and if it is assumed "that a thousand lines can be comfortably read in about an hour (alliterative long-lines would take about twice as long), it follows that each of these poems probably would have been read in one sitting" (1968:36-7). Several poems are about twice that length and they may have been divided in half and read in two instalments. Mehl has found a passage in *The Seege or Batayle of Troy* to support his thesis. In this poem of about two thousand lines there is in one of the manuscripts a passage (ll.980-83) that indicates the half-way point and that includes a short blessing and, significantly, a call for drinks. This clearly suggests a break in the delivery. There are similar passages to be found in other poems, and on the whole the longer romances are far less close-knit than the shorter ones and are clearly divided into separate episodes, some of which could, if necessary, be omitted or read separately. In Mehl's view, the length of a poem has implications for its oral delivery, which in turn affects the structure of the poem.

In Mehl's classification *HD* comes under the heading of the 'longer romances': its length, 3001 lines, would call for delivery in three instalments (possibly two), but it is not easy to find more or less natural breaks after approximately a third and two thirds of the poem. On the other hand, the structure of the narrative suggests a division into episodes (indicated by changes in setting: England – Denmark – England – Denmark – England), but all these episodes are necessary for the plot, which would become unintelligible if they were omitted. Earlier, in the discussion of the word *spelle* (l.338), we have noted that this line separates the two introductory episodes, and the ten lines preceding l.338 round off the episode set in England. In this line 338 the poet directly addresses his audience, and with this line the story shifts from England to Denmark. At the next shift of setting there is a similar address to the audience: *As ye shulen nou forthward lere, / Yf that ye wilen per-to here* (ll.731-2: 'As you shall learn as the story proceeds, if you will listen to it'). With this line the story moves back to England: the landing of Grim in Lincolnshire. When the poet next addresses his audience, a change of setting has already taken place: *Þat sholen ye forthward ful wel leren, / Yif þat ye wile þe storie heren* (ll.1640-41: 'That you shall learn indeed as the story proceeds, if you will listen to it'). The difficulty here is that one leaf has been cut out of the MS, containing 180 lines (1444-1625), and on this particular leaf the change of setting from England to Denmark must have been effected. At the fourth and final change of setting the audience is only indirectly addressed by the poet (there is no *ye* as in the other changes): *Of Grim bidde ich na more spelle.— But whan Godrich herde telle, ...* (ll.2530-31: 'I ask leave to tell of Grim no more. — But when Godrich heard tell ...'). In the lines immediately preceding, Havelok, still in Denmark at the time, has sworn to found a priory for the salvation of Grim's soul, in the town where Grim was buried and which bears his name (ll.2528-9). The poet then continues with the lines just quoted, and what Godrich had heard was that Havelok, now King of Denmark, had arrived in England to claim the throne. This transition from Denmark to England is therefore less clearly marked than the other transitions, but it is hinted at by the poet's intervention.

There are, then, five distinct episodes in the poem, and all the transitions between them are marked by the poet addressing the audience. However, none of these transitions occurs after groups of approximately one thousand lines, which Mehl considers the standard length for delivery in one sitting, as we have seen. It may well be that the break between the third and fourth episodes, occurring in the portion of the poem now lost, was explicitly referred to by the poet, a break that would have come at approximately the half-way point in the story. This would suggest a reading of the poem in two sittings, and the second sitting would in that case have involved the final two episodes, both of which are a kind of climax in the narrative, the fourth episode dealing with Havelok winning the crown of Denmark and with the execution of the false guardian Godard, the fifth episode with Havelok winning the crown of England and with the execution of the false guardian Godrich.

The oral delivery has affected not only the structure of the poem, which is, as we have seen, made up of five distinct episodes, but it has also affected the development of the plot, which we shall examine in some detail, but it may not be inappropriate to give a brief synopsis of the poem first.

The story of *HD* is the story of two dispossessed young royal orphans, a prince in Denmark, Havelok, and a princess in England, Goldeboru. After their fathers, both of whom are depicted as good kings, have died in the prime of their lives, Havelok and Goldeboru are each left in the hands of a supposedly good guardian, who proves treacherous, however, in wishing to usurp the throne. In the end Havelok vanquishes both the Danish and the English usurpers and recovers the two kingdoms for himself and Goldeboru, who has become his wife.

The plot of *HD* shows, according to Hanning (1967:588) three common elements of romance plots: (1) the hero's movement from loss to recovery—this is the most common element of the romance plot, and it also covers the device of the discovery of 'real identity'; (2) the hero's development from immaturity or faultiness to maturity and perfection; and (3) a love relationship which unites the hero (in his deprived and/or developing state) and a heroine who has also been the victim of deprivation or other injustice. These three plot elements which are clearly interrelated have been unified by the poet into a narrative with an artistic structure, as we shall see.

On the level of the plot the oral delivery of the poem manifests itself in the recurrence of a number of symbols and acts which are central to the theme of the poem and to the development of the plot. This recurrence is frequently realized by means of verbal repetitions, which the poet employs for a twofold purpose: through these repetitions he not only provides the audience with easy points of reference, enabling them to link a given passage to an earlier passage, but through these repetitions he can also communicate to his audience the importance of what they have just heard or are about to hear. In other words, the verbal repetitions, and recurrences in general, for that matter, have both a unifying function (with regard to structure) and an emphatic function (with regard to plot and narrative).

This twofold purpose is illustrated by the first two episodes of *HD*, which deal with similar events in England and Denmark (for an outline of these episodes, see the discussion of the word *spelle* above), and which therefore constitute the first instance of repetition on a large scale. The first episode narrates how a young and helpless heiress is stripped of her rights (and thereby of her future) by a strong and wicked adult[8], and the second episode narrates the same

---

[8] Note that at the end of the first episode we have yet to meet the hero of the poem. This may seem strange in the light of the poet's announcement in the Prologue that *þe tale of Hauelok is i-maked* (1.5: 'the story is about Havelok'), yet we shall demonstrate that Havelok figures prominently, though indirectly of course, in this episode.

process with regard to a young and helpless heir. Why did the poet opt for this double statement of misery and misfortune? We have already given a possible answer when we said that the opening episodes make the audience side with the hero against his adversaries, and in this way the poet assures himself of the continued attention of his audience, since they have now become involved in the story. But there is more to these first two episodes. The double statement of misfortune serves to emphasize the contrast between the helplessness of youth and the power of adulthood, and Hanning (1967:590) sees in this contrast a direct reference to two of "the central movements of the Havelok story", the movement from loss to recovery and the complementary movement from youth to maturity (mentioned above as two common elements of romance plots): "By linking youth and loss twice in quick succession ..., *Havelok the Dane* unmistakably announces the thematic interests which control its narrative progress." The movement from loss to recovery is marked off by two almost identical lines, the first symbolizing Havelok's loss, the second his recovery. The first of these lines occurs when the wicked Earl Godard has slaughtered Havelok's two sisters and is about to do the same to Havelok, who, kneeling before Godard, asks for mercy, saying

> Manrede, louerd, biddi you!   (484)
>
> (Feudal homage, lord, I offer you!)

With these words Havelok surrenders his sovereignty and becomes a vassal to the earl, whom he now recognizes as his lord. By offering homage to Godard, Havelok symbolically (and therefore implicitly) denies his social identity as heir to the Danish throne, which in turn leads to his explicit loss of personal identity in leaving Denmark to grow up as a fisherman's son in England (cf. Hanning, 1967:592). Line 484 thus symbolizes the low point of the story, and it is to be related to the second occurrence of this particular line in the poem, slightly modified but with essentially the same meaning: *Manred, louerd, bede y pe* (1.2172: 'Feudal homage, lord, I offer you'). Here the person addressed is Havelok, and the words are spoken by Ubbe, a great Danish earl who had been a close friend of Havelok's father, King Birkabeyn. Having seen Havelok's birth-marks (on which we comment below), this Ubbe recognizes him as *"Birkabeynes sone"* (1.2150: 'Birkabeyn's son') and realizes that he is the rightful heir to the Danish throne (*"he is hise eyr"*, 1.2157: 'he is his [i.e. Bir-kabeyn's] heir'); then Ubbe and his men fall on their knees and offer homage to Havelok with the words of line 2172, which is therefore symbolic of the moment of recovery, and at this point the main action of *HD* is completed. The moment of recovery does not have to coincide with Havelok's coronation as King of Denmark, because he was not yet king when he offered homage to Godard. Note that the order of the final steps towards the moment of recovery is the exact opposite of that of the consequences of the loss:

A. the loss
   1. Havelok's feudal homage to Godard, i.e. his giving up his sovereignty;
   2. his loss of social identity;
   3. his loss of personal identity.
B. the recovery
   1. Havelok's recovery of personal identity (1.2150);
   2. his recovery of social identity (1.2157);
   3. Ubbe's feudal homage to Havelok (1.2172), restoring Havelok's sovereignty.

Note also that about half-way between lines 484 and 2172 there is a first indication that Havelok is well on the way to recover what he had lost. It occurs after Havelok has fled with his wife Goldeboru from Lincoln to Grimsby and is received by Grim's children who surrender themselves to him: *Þou maght us boþe selle and yeue; / Þou maght us boþe yeue and selle, / With-þat þou wilt here dwelle* (ll.1218-20: 'You might both sell and give us [i.e. into slavery]; you might both give and sell us, on condition that you stay here'). They also turn over all their property to him: *Bi-leue her, louerd, and al be þin!* (1.1228: 'Stay here, lord, and everything will be yours!'), and next they accept him as their lord:*Þou shalt ben louerd, þou shalt ben syre, / And we sholen seruen þe and hire.* (ll. 1229-30: 'You shall be lord, you shall be sir, and we shall serve you and her [i.e. Goldeboru]'.) However, Havelok's installation as head of the Grim household is more than a first sign of the process of recovery being well under way: it also points forward to Havelok's eventual corona-tion as King of Denmark, since the Grim household, a Danish family in exile in England, symbolically stands for the Danish nation, and their acceptance of Havelok as *paterfamilias* thus has symbolic signi-ficance. This scene also points backwards, as it echoes the words spoken by Grim after he had witnessed the first manifestations of Havelok's 'birth-marks' and prophesied

> þis ure eir
> Þat shal ben louerd of Denemark,
> He shal ben king, strong and stark;
> He shal hauen in his hand
> Al Denemark and Engeland.   (606-10)

(This is our heir who shall be lord of Denmark, he shall be king, strong and stout; he shall have in his power all of Denmark and England.)

And Grim then does homage to Havelok:

> Louerd, haue merci
> Of me, and Leue, þat is me bi!
> Louerd, we aren boþe þine,
> Þine cherles, þine hine.   (617-20)

(Lord have mercy on me and on Leue, who is standing beside me! Lord, we are both yours, your thralls and your servants.)

Thus, the homage which Grim offers the child Havelok is as it were reaffirmed by Grim's children when they do homage to the grown-up Havelok, and it is this difference in Havelok's age that makes this reaffirmation more effective and symbolically significant.

The repetition of 1.484 in 1.2172 and the reverse patterning of the elements involved in the processes of loss and recovery betray the skill of a great story-teller, one who knew how to relate plot to structure. This is equally apparent from the way in which he handles the second thematic movement, the hero's development from an immature youth to a mature adult. Such a process of growth must be gradual, and therefore it cannot have the clear beginning and ending of the first thematic movement. Consequently it must consist of a series of recurring incidents, each of them symbolzing a particular phase in this process of growth to adulthood. Hanning (1967:594) has identified these recurring incidents with symbolic meaning, which are of three kinds: (1) feasts; (2) feats of strength; and (3) revelations of Havelok's birth-marks. They are interrelated in the sense that a feast often follows a feat of strength and/or a revelation of birth-marks, and this interrelation is further evidence of the poet's skill.

In medieval romance feasts and, more generally, dinners, often have a particular symbolic function.[9] In *HD* there are no fewer than six occasions on which food is consumed, and although the first two of them are hardly feasts, since they lack the ceremonial and social aspects inherent in a feast, they all occur at crucial moments in the story and signal important stages in the hero's development to adulthood. In this series of meals and feasts there is a kind of progression that runs parallel to Havelok's growth to adulthood: each meal is more important than the previous one, and this is reflected in the food served at each meal—just as the meals become more and more important, the food becomes richer and richer. The sixth and final meal in the series, Havelok's coronation feast in England, is described by the poet in only three lines (ll.2948-50), which seems to indicate that the poet regarded this sixth feast as relatively unimportant (cf. his elaborate treatment of Havelok's coronation feast in Denmark, ll.2320-45), no doubt because it falls outside the poem's thematic movement, the hero's development to adulthood and maturity having been completed with the coronation feast in Denmark. Table I, which is based on Hanning (1967:594-98), summarizes this series of meals and feasts and specifies the symbolic significance of each meal or feast to the hero's development to adulthood.

The second series of recurring incidents that is symbolic of Havelok's growth to adulthood is that of his feats of strength, which he performs on three occasions. Havelok's strength is repeatedly mentioned (e.g. l.829: *For he was strong*; ll.988-90: *He was boþe*

---

[9] In *Sir Gawain and the Green Knight*, for instance, each of the two dramatic movements making up the plot, the Beheading Game and the Exchange of Gifts, has a dinner or a series of dinners as the setting for its initial or central action. In the case of the Beheading Game it is the Christmas dinner at Arthur's court, the first course of which had hardly been served when the Green Knight came riding into the hall at Camelot (ll.135-36). The Green Knight's challenge for *a Crystemas gomen* (l.283: 'a Christmas game') creates a dramatic tension which is only partially relieved by his subsequent beheading, and therefore interferes with the joyous atmosphere of the Christmas dinner. (This is not the place to go into the symbolic significance of the relation between the dinner and the challenge and beheading.) Similarly, the Exchange of Gifts, agreed upon by Gawain and his host Bertilak for the duration of Gawain's stay at Hautdesert, takes place immediately before dinner on three consecutive nights (ll.1372-1401, 1623-57, 1932-56). These dinners serve to emphasize the fellowship between host and guest, just as the Exchange of Gifts is a gesture of fellowship (see Burrow, 1965:95, and Aertsen, 1987:98-100).

FEAST	LINES	SETTING	OCCASION	SYMBOLIC SIGNIFICANCE
1	634-56	Grim's cottage (in Denmark)	after the planned murder of H. by Grim is prevented by the first revelation of the two signs of his royal descent; Grim accepts H. as his lord	the first concrete sign that H. has stepped back from the brink of death; the feast/meal acts to restore his famished body
2	921-30	the kitchen of the Earl's Cook in Lincoln	after H. is hired by the Cook to carry his baskets of fish	H.'s first independent and competitive steps in the world; again the feast/meal acts to restore his famished body
3	1237-46	the house of Grim's children at Grimsby	after H. is accepted by Grim's children as their lord	central function in the story: points back to Grim's acceptance of H. (see 1) and forward to H.'s coronation as King of Denmark (see 5)
4	1714-29	the castle of Ubbe, a Danish earl and close friend of H.'s father	H., pretending to be a merchant, is granted permission by Ubbe to make a living in his district, gives the earl a gold ring (cf. note 9); Ubbe suspects that H. is more than he claims to be and invites H. and his company to a dinner	H. is back in Denmark and is on the threshold of the victory toward which he had been maturing since the first night and meal in Grim's cottage
5	2340-45	not identified in the poem—probably Ubbe's castle	H.'s coronation banquet, preceded by games and tournaments, songs and minstrelsy	this banquet highlights the series of feasts: H., now King of Denmark, has regained all that he had lost earlier
6	2948-50	London	H.'s coronation feast in England	relatively unimportant: falls outside the poem's thematic movement (see text)

Table I

Meals and Feasts in *HD*

[H. = Havelok]

stark and strong; / In Engelond was non his per / Of strengþe 'He was both stout and strong; in England no one was his equal in strength'), and Havelok has thus fulfilled what Grim had prophesied about him after the revelation of his birth-marks in Grim's hut: *he shal ben king, strong and stark* (1.608: 'he shall be king, stout and strong'). Table II lists these feats of strength and specifies their symbolic significance. The many references to Havelok's strength are what one might expect of a romance hero, but in his growth to adulthood it is not sufficient that he should be strong—in the contests and fights in which he engages he should come out the winner: that is what one expects of a future king and that is why 1.608 is a key line in the poem. Note that, as in the series of feasts, there is a kind of progression in Havelok's feats of strength: when he first fights his way to the job of basket carrier for the Earl's Cook, he overcomes "nine or ten" rivals (1. 871), the next day he beats as many as sixteen of them (1.890) and the number of thieves who attack Bernard's house is given as 61 in 1.1918. As the opposition increases, Havelok's feats become more and more impressive. Note also that in the descriptions of the victorious Havelok the poet emphasizes not only his physical strength but also his social qualities—gentleness, generosity and justice: 11.930-44 describe his physical strength, 11.945-58 his social qualities (cf. 1.945: *Of alle men was he mest meke* 'Of all men he was gentlest'). The poet links this description of Havelok's social qualities to the description of King Athelwold in the first introductory episode: 11.955-6 (*Him loueden alle, stille and bolde, / Knihtes, children, yunge and olde* 'Everybody, shy and bold, loved him, knights, children, young and old') echo 1.30 (*Him louede yong, him louede olde* 'Young and old loved him'), as if to indicate that Havelok has by now developed the qualities of a good and just king. When the poet speaks of Havelok's fame after the games at Lincoln, he combines these two aspects into a single line: *Hu he was strong and ek ful meke* (1.1066: 'how strong he was, and also how very gentle'). Finally it is worth noting that there is a subtle touch of irony in the passage dealing with Godrich's decision to have Goldeboru marry Havelok: it was not only to fulfil his promise to the dying Athelwold that Goldeboru was to marry "the best, the fairest, and also the strongest man alive" (11.198-200) but also to ensure himself and his son after him of the English throne (11.1073-76), yet Goldeboru's marriage to Havelok is *not* disgraceful, and it does *not* ensure Godrich of the throne, it has precisely the opposite effect, as it in fact leads to his downfall.

FEAT	LINES	SETTING	OCCASION	SYMBOLIC SIGNIFICANCE
1a 1b	871-78 889-92	Lincoln	pushing aside his competitors ("nine or ten" the first day, "sixteen" the next) for a job as carrier of baskets of fish for the Earl's Cook	this feat wins H. food in a time of famine (his second feast) and a steady job (his first independent steps in the world); the poet also stresses his social qualities (ll.945-58; see text)
2	979-1058	the games at Lincoln	ordered by the Cook to compete, H. wins the contest by "putting the stone" further than anyone else	this feat wins H. great fame (ll.1059-66); when Godrich hears of it, he makes Goldeboru marry H. (see text for details and for the irony involved)
3	1766-1919	at the house of Bernard, the magistrate in the town where Ubbe lives	H. is sent to Bernard by Ubbe to make sure that he and his wife will not be harmed, but Bernard's house is attacked by a gang of sixty thieves; H. kills then all with the help of the sons of Grim	Bernard, telling Ubbe of H.'s feat, emphasizes that H. saved his life and goods (ll.1974f, 2002-5); taking H. back to his own castle, Ubbe discovers H.'s real identity during the night, after witnessing H.'s birth-marks

Table II: Havelok's Feats of Strength

	LINES	SETTING	OCCASION	SYMBOLIC SIGNIFICANCE
1	588-605	Grim's cottage in Denmark	Grim is about to carry out Godard's order to kill H.	it saves his life, discloses H.'s real identity; Grim prohesies that H. shall be king of Denmark and England
2	1251-57	bedroom in the house of Grim's children	after the feast (no.3) H. and Goldeboru go to bed	it reveals his identity to his wife, who has the marks interpreted by an angel who repeats Grim's prophecy
3	2090-2147	Ubbe's castle	during the night following feat no.3	it reveals his identity to Ubbe, who does homage to him and dubs him a knight; H. is then made King of Denmark

Table III: Manifestations of Havelok's Birth-Marks

The third series of recurring incidents that, together with the feasts and the feats of strength, symbolize Havelok's growth to adulthood is that of the revelation of his *kyne-mark* (1.604: 'sign of his royal rank', i.e. the mark on his right shoulder) and the flame from his mouth, which are commonly referred to as Havelok's 'birth-marks'. There are three occasions on which these birth-marks are revealed so as to disclose the true identity of the hero, and they are listed in Table III, together with their symbolic significance. Note that on two of the three occasions the revelation of Havelok's birth-marks is followed by the prophecy that he shall be king of Denmark and England—first it is Grim who says so (ll.608-10), and then it is the angel interpreting the birth-marks for Goldeboru (ll. 1265-74; in the angel's prophecy there is yet another instance of verbal repetition in the poem, as 1.1271 repeats 1.608 verbatim). On the third occasion that Havelok's identity is disclosed Ubbe does homage to Havelok (which marks the moment of recovery) and then promises that Havelok shall be king of Denmark (1.2178)—this time it is not a prophecy because Ubbe at once takes the necessary steps to fulfil his promise.

The intricate plot with its two thematic movements and with the interrelationships between the series of recurring incidents making up the second movement, and the verbal repetitions throughout the poem show that the poet was a great story-teller; if his verse had been of the same high quality, *HD* would have been one of the finest Middle English poems.

REFERENCES

Aertsen, H. (1987). *Play in Middle English. A Contribution to Word Field Theory.* Amsterdam: Free University Press.
Baugh, A.C. (1948). *A Literary History of England.* London: Routledge and Kegan Paul.
Bennett, J.A.W. (1986). *Middle English Literature.* Ed. D. Gray. The Oxford History of English Literature, Vol. I, Part 2. Oxford: O.U.P.
Burrow, J.A. (1965). *A Reading of* Sir Gawain and the Green Knight. London: Routledge and Kegan Paul.
Creek, H.L. (1915). The Author of *Havelok the Dane. Englische Studien* 48. 193-212.
Everett, D. (1955). A Characterisation of the English Mediaeval Romances. In: *Essays on Middle English Literature.* Ed. P. Kean. Oxford: O.U.P. 1-22.

French, W.H. and C.B. Hale (eds.) (1964). *Middle English Metrical Romances*. 2
    Vols. New York: Russell and Russell. (1st publ., 1930.)
Hanning, R.W. (1967). *Havelok the Dane*: Structure, Symbols, Meaning. *Studies
    in Philology* 64. 586-605.
Holthausen, F. (ed.) (1928). *Havelok*. 3rd ed. Alt- und Mittelenglische Texte I.
    Heidelberg: Carl Winter. (1st ed., 1901.)
Ker, W.P. (1907). Metrical Romances, 1200-1500. I. In: *The Cambridge History
    of English Literature*. Ed. A.W. Ward and A.R. Waller. Vol. I. Cambridge:
    C.U.P. 277-300.
Mehl, D. (1968). *The Middle English Romances of the Thirteenth and Fourteenth
    Centuries*. London: Routledge and Kegan Paul.
Pearsall, D. (1965). The Development of Middle English Romance. *Mediaeval
    Studies* 27. 91-116.
Schmidt, A.V.C. and N. Jacobs (eds.) (1980). *Medieval English Romances*. 2
    Vols. London: Hodder and Stoughton.
Schofield, W.H. (1906). *English Literature from the Norman Conquest to
    Chaucer*. London: Macmillan.
Skeat, W.W. and K. Sisam (eds.) (1915). *The Lay of Havelok the Dane*. 2nd rev.
    ed. Oxford: O.U.P. (1st ed., 1902.)
Smithers, G.V. (ed.) (1987). *Havelok*. Oxford: O.U.P.
Staines, D. (1976). Havelok the Dane: A Thirteenth-Century Handbook for
    Princes. *Speculum* 51. 602-23.
Strohm, P. (1971). *Storie, Spelle, Geste, Romaunce, Tragedie*: Generic
    Distinctions in the Middle English Troy Narratives. *Speculum* 46. 348-59.
Weiss, J. (1969). Structure and Characterisation in *Havelok the Dane*. *Speculum*
    44. 247-57.
Wilson, R.M. (1968). *Early Middle English Literature*. 3rd ed. London: Methuen.
    (1st ed., 1939.)

FLORIS AND BLAUNCHEFLOUR
TO INDULGE THE FANCY AND TO HEAR OF LOVE

N.H.G.E. VELDHOEN
(University of Leiden)

J.W.H. Atkins (1907:301) prefaces his discussion of the Middle English metrical romances by pointing out that

> the *raison d' être* of the romances is of a secular kind. It was felt to be good to indulge the fancy and to hear of love, and so legendary and historical narratives and cheerful love-stories were, from time to time, related with no other motive than the telling of a good tale.

Although *Floris and Blauncheflour* (henceforth *Fl & Bl*) is perhaps not, in the strictest sense, a romance—it is not a story of knight-errantry—yet the story of the two young lovers is told in the conventional narrative technique of the genre of the romance of chivalry. And Atkins' well-considered words will appear to apply particularly to this tale.

The point about the genre of *Fl & Bl* needs to be made because for the modern reader, conditioned by the modern novel or short story with their realistic verisimilitude, the kind of narrative to which *Fl & Bl* belongs is not immediately accessible. The story may be compelling enough, but the full impact of the medieval English rendering of this story will not be grasped unless one is ready and willing to accept a high degree of formality in it, which constitutes its own peculiar logic and significance.

Romances are stories of public life: they portray the age's ideals of life, of men and women, of what makes life significant. Underlying the romances is the assumption that rituals, when performed in the proper manner, add significance to life, or rather bring out the significance that life had in the theological culture of those days. And this is not only true for religious or courtly rituals, nor only for public or special rituals, but as much for what we would consider private or common rituals. For them such distinctions are immaterial. Swooning in public or in private, eating, asking the way, playing chess, as rituals properly performed, add as much significance to the life portrayed as the selection of a queen or the Christian marriage-ceremony.

This medieval sense of ceremony, i.e. formality as a way of celebrating significance in life, is reflected in the formality of construction of these tales. In *Fl & Bl* the formality is immediately apparent in the ritualistic repetitions: there are several innkeepers, several guides, several obstacles to be overcome, several disguises, even the game of chess is to be played three times. Also words and lines are repeated in the same ritualistic way: from the characteristic *vnnepes* ('reluctantly', ll.63 and 153) to describe Floris' father, to Floris' equally characteristic reaction when he is offered food:

> Mi þouʒt is, on alle wise,
> Mochel on mi marchaundise,
> And ʒit þat is mi meste wo
> ʒif ich hit finde and schal forgo.   (503-6)

(My thinking is in every way much engaged upon my merchandise, and yet that is my greatest anxiety, if I should find it and be obliged to do without it.)

These lines are repeated almost verbatim in ll.589-94.[1]

But the formality, the sense of ceremony in this kind of narrative, also accounts for such details as seem necessary for the plot: the second ring, the details of food eaten (ll.569-76), the blankets only pulled down a little to ascertain the sexes of the lovers in bed (ll.1059-62), the Emir marrying Clarice in the end.

Where we finally need this notion of formality most, where we need to see and accept the absolute dominance of the medieval sense of ceremony, is in our reading of those details which, in a modern narrative, should be noted as inconsistent in the story: the Oriental and pagan Emir is given West European chivalric paraphernalia. This unnatural despot has his city guarded by knights; he allows himself to be guided by a council of barons, placing chivalric honour over despotic judgment; he dubs Floris a knight and even administers a Christian marriage.

In other words, the spirit or mood in which we are required to enjoy and interpret such stories is that with which we also approach fairy tales and folktales. They have the "feel" of the dream world: in

---

[1] All quotations from *Fl & Bl* have been taken from the edition by Taylor (1927).

a dream one can fly, and that causes no surprise, yet the feeling is memorable. And they have the logic of ritual games: the logic that makes us avoid the black lines with our feet when stepping across a zebra crossing. It is the symbolic logic of life experienced as basic desires and fears, and the ritual patterns ensuing from that.

In such narratives we are not shocked by what in modern stories should be considered as cruelty. In *Sir Gawain and the Green Knight* the beheading game does not unduly worry us. Neither need we be surprised in *Fl & Bl* to find Floris' father so murderously inclined. When on two occasions he proposes to have Blauncheflour killed (ll.45-51 and 141), he is speaking as the King who must insist on a fitting marriage-partner for his successor. And apart from this ritual aspect of his conduct, he is at the same time acting out the part of the father as rival or restrainer of his son's maturing sensuality. It is interesting to notice that by the side of the father's cruel effectiveness it is Floris'mother, or rather the King's wife, whose role it is to introduce more civilized alternatives. She proposes to send Floris away for some time *Þat he lese not his honour / For þe mayden Blauncheflour* (ll.57-8: 'in order that he will not lose his honour because of the young girl Blauncheflour') and later proposes the ruse of selling the girl away and pretending that she is dead (ll.144-52). It is characteristic that in both cases the King submits *vnnepes* ('reluctantly', ll.63 and 153), just as in similar instances later on he submits reluctantly to his wife and son: *Sen it may noon other be* (l.322: 'since it may not be otherwise') and *Seth it is soo, / Seþ þou wylt noon other doo* (ll.351-2: 'since that is how it is, since you will not do otherwise'). So love as a civilizing influence on the harsh man's world of public interest is shown to gain a hard-won victory. Similarly in the end the emir appears easily moved by the young lovers and ready to have a civilized trial rather than summary justice (ll. 1109-30).

The Queen's loving influence does not stop at civilizing her husband's attitude and thereby granting full development to their son. She is also shown literally to give life to her son when she prevents his suicide at Blauncheflour's alleged grave. And symbolically she also gives life to Blauncheflour by opening the grave and showing that the girl is still alive (ll.308-40). This ultimate act of love wins the field for the lovers.

Fl & Bl is undeniably a story of love, although John Stevens rightly remarks (1973:44) that, in contrast to other romances, love here is not "all dark passion" or "merely businesslike":

> Amongst the English romances which seem to concede
> most to amorous ideals is *Fl & Bl*. But the concessions
> are more to sentiment than to *amour*. (...) Floris and
> Blancheflur are counters in a game of sentiments.

Every reader knows the sentiments of Ideal Love. We all know
what to expect and wish for. And that is dramatized in the romances.
But first and foremost we are aware of the obstacles, of our fears
and misgivings. And those are dramatized primarily in the romances,
and give them their shape of a series of conflicts. Our hopes are
reflected in the fact that the hero invariably wins through. But the
interest lies in the fears portrayed in action. These are the real points
of recognition and of identification. Floris' parents and the gatekeeper and the Emir are in a way more real to our experience than
Floris himself can ever be.

The love-interest in the Middle English romances operates on
various levels. One level is that of strongly felt human relationships.
On another, love is an ennobling and civilizing force. On again
another love is the inspiration to transcend one's present self by
means of action on behalf of a lady. This is love as part of the
process of growing up, of growing away from self-centredness and
mere self-assertion towards a civilized social identity. *Fl & Bl* shows
that achieved love leads to social integrity: Floris and Blauncheflour's first free acts are acts of loyalty to the other characters involved. Floris loyally protects his 'man', the gatekeeper, from the
Emir's wrath (ll.1245-50)—appropriately before he himself becomes
the Emir's 'man', thus avoiding a clash of loyalties—and Blauncheflour intercedes for her trusted friend Clarice, achieving final harmony in the form of a marriage between Clarice and the Emir (ll.
1277-9).

In the romance-manner of story-telling all the action and all
the other characters are to be seen as reflecting the development of
the protagonist. Therefore it is in Floris that we see the "education"
that leads to the perfect love achieved in the end. And typically, his
love-education follows the pattern of what from classical antiquity
had been recognized as man's fundamental desires: his *libido*. That
libido had been split into three kinds or levels: the *libido sciendi* ('the
desire to know'), the *libido dominandi* ('the desire to dominate'), and
the *libido sentiendi* ('the desire to feel, to be emotionally involved').
We can recognise the *libido sciendi* in the emphasis on Floris' going
to school and on his being so dependent on instructions from others

to achieve his ends. Floris receives directions and is taught the tricks—here in the form of plots and ruses—how to cope with "life". The *libido dominandi* is brought out in his many struggles against repression, in which he successively overcomes his parents, the gate-keeper, and finally, in a sense, the Emir. And in a love-story such as *Fl & Bl* the *libido sentiendi* is dominantly present. Floris' quest for his chosen love-partner is a quest for integrity, for a place and an identity in the grown-up world. The *libido sentiendi* is brought out by Floris' trying to achieve a pattern of relatedness and mutual loyalties. The enforcing of the truth at Blaunchefour's tomb and the struggle over who shall have the protective ring are the dramatic highlights of this narrative vein.

Having established the basic pattern of the ideal experience, there now remains to be seen of what nature the characters are in this for-mal world, and what the nature is of the "adventures" to which they are submitted.

We see Floris growing from child to independent man and master of men. That this is a difficult and painful process is illus-trated by the fact that on seven different occasions on the way Floris does the unmanly thing: he weeps, either for frustration or fear or joy (ll.15-17; 83; 270; 847; 932; 947; 1134). This pattern of growth might have made for dramatic variety and tragic depth, as it had done in the epic narratives that preceded romances in time. But neither is to be found. The hero is a stereotype 'flat' protagonist, for the interest lies in the action, not in the character of the hero. He is an embodiment of virtue or of growth towards virtue. His story can-not be tragic, because if he dies, the virtue he embodies perishes with him, whereas romance sets out to show the virtue literally for what it is worth. This does not mean that there is nothing explorative to romances. Yet the character of the hero is 'flat'. The tensions and conflicting motives underlying the ideals are brought out by the action, not by dramatic conflicts within the character. The action is the full drama of the portrayed ideal, and the various characters, including the hero, personify various facets of the complex experi-ence of trying to attain that ideal. The hero enacts the striving towards the pure ideal, while the other characters are representatives of the checks imposed by 'reality' and by the co-existence of other fundamental passions. Because the protagonist is the example or 'type' aimed at, all characters other than the protagonist are only important in relation to the protagonist, not in relation to each other. They 'are' the action.

The character of Floris is a *persona*, a 'mask'. We do not see an individual character experiencing 'reality' in his own particular way. The fact that he has a name does not make him an individual. In Floris we see an ignorant and dependent young boy winning through to a socially acceptable position. And we see him also developing. While he has to be shown his way most of the time, we see him taking the initiative twice, at crucial points: after the ruse of Blaunche-flour's faked tomb has been exploded, Floris himself decides that he shall set out to find the girl, and he states his own terms of how he proposes to travel and what he will take with him; and ultimately it is the spontaneous act of endlessly exchanging the protective ring that overcomes the Emir. And yet Floris remains more or less the ignorant helpless child he was from the start.

This apparent inconsistency of a character showing development and yet remaining largely what he was from the beginning is typical of all romance heroes. They "go through the motions", but only to show that, and how, the ideal they represent overcomes all tests. The tests are not really moments of doubt, but elements that serve to define the nature of the ideal portrayed in action.

The term 'flat' suits the other characters in this narrative better. They are static: they cannot be 'educated'. They are representations of the perennial fears attendant upon Floris' ideal social personality. Floris' father and the gatekeeper and the Emir introduce into the action all these uncivilized desires that are incompatible with what Floris stands for. They constitute the primitive, uncontrolled and animal parts of the human being against which the protagonist is tested. They are the antagonists proper to Floris: they define him.

On his way to find himself, the ideal lover Floris overcomes three antagonists to that ideal: his father, the gatekeeper, and the Emir. His father represses his striving for integrity in the form of union with his appropriate partner Blauncheflour on the grounds of social conventions. These conventions of the impropriety of marriage between people of unequal birth—here pushed to the absolute of murder to prevent that—are represented as unfitting for the type of love that *Fl & Bl* idealizes.

The gatekeeper represses Floris' progress towards the achievement of his love on the grounds of a peculiar symbolic rivalry, which I will discuss later on. He has the peacock appearance of the typical rival lover: *Þe porter is proud wiþalle; / Euerich dai he goþ*

in palle (ll.679-80: 'besides, the gatekeeper is proud: he is dressed in
a rich robe every day'. Moreover, he is portrayed as jealous:

> Wel sone he wil come to þe
> And aske what mister man þou be
> And ber vpon þe felonie,
> And saie þou art comen þe tour aspie.   (753-6)

(Very soon he will come up to you and ask what business you have
there, and accuse you of malicious intentions, saying you have come
to spy on the tower.)

To this Floris is advised to reply with the meekness befitting the true
lover: *Þou shalt answeren him swetelich / And speke to him wel
mildelich* (ll.757-8: 'you must answer him graciously and speak to
him meekly').

The medieval ideal lover will especially have to overcome the
Emir, because the uncivilized type of love represented by him does
certainly not fit the European ideal of the day. The Emir is not
chivalrous to his ladies, whom he buys in the first place. He would be
well described by the modern term 'male chauvinist pig': his 'love' is
all lust and, one assumes, businesslike procreation, without any sense
of relationship towards his partner. And that would be unacceptable
to the mainly female audiences of Eleanor of Aquitaine's generation.

Quite appropriately Floris' antagonists are all male, because
the checks to the ideal he portrays are aspects of the male psyche.
The female characters in *Fl & Bl*, for their part, are manifestations
of various aspects of the nature of Woman, at least of the idea of
Woman in a man's mind. That idea appears to be mainly a set of
complements to his own nature. Such complements can, in general,
as easily enhance the beneficial as the malevolent aspects of his
world. But in the love-romance *Fl & Bl* the female characters
typically represent the positive influence on the male world. Floris'
women add a whole range of experience of feminine virtue to the
ideal action.

Blauncheflour is, throughout, a young lover's projection of an
ideal love. She is from the beginning inseparably part of him, as his
refusal to go to school—that is, to start on social life—without her
bears out (ll.15-24). Their separation illustrates that a sense of
separateness and social obstacles will have to be overcome before a
full union can be achieved. The hero will have to learn, will have to
gain wider experience, before the union can become socially rele-

vant. Yet in the end Blauncheflour is still the ideal young love who literally forgets the whole world—the necessity to keep up her duties towards the Emir—when she is with her lover (ll.979-1039). Also ideally, she had remained absolutely faithful to Floris, to the point of contemplating suicide rather than being another man's wife (ll.907-20).

Further details of his experience of woman Floris encounters in his mother. On the one hand she shares with Blauncheflour's mother a 'malevolent' role in maintaining the falsehood of the girl's death, which provides Floris with a reason to leave her as well as his father. But on the other hand Floris' mother is a manifestation of the virtue of love. Her role is to civilize her husband and their relationship with their child, thereby setting their son free to start out on his own. Thus to the hero's experience and to the story's scope she adds the fundamental notion that love is an ennobling force and that it can overcome all obstacles in its way.

Blauncheflour's friend and confidante Clarice adds to Floris' experience a woman's capacity for devoted loyalty, as also for clever subterfuge, when she tells the Emir that Blauncheflour slept late because she had been praying for him all night (ll.1005-14). She parallels Floris' mother, who also risked displeasure and resorted to subterfuge—the suggestion to sell Blauncheflour away and simulate her death was hers—to achieve what she held to be a more civilized order of affairs. There is, therefore, poetic justice in Clarice being married to the Emir, another uncouth husband whom, no doubt, she is to civilize, thus creating a neat end to this story of integrity. The formal pattern of ennobling love thus reigns supreme, against all improbabilities.

The other characters in *Fl & Bl* are devices to help enact the above pattern. The good men and women along the road serve as guides to Floris on his way to private happiness which is the social good. The gatekeeper's opposite number on the right side, Daris, is the clearest example of the disinterested guide, who has nothing to gain but the common good, which in terms of this romance is Floris' union with Blauncheflour.

The frequency of this guidance may be worth notice. Three times Floris receives information and guidance on the road: first from a landlady (ll.428-39), then from the men of Babylon, the 'talk of the town' (ll.465-76), and finally again from a landlord, another member of that life-sustaining and rest-providing guild (ll.527-36). Then he is three times passed on into other hands, by his last host to

Daris (ll.549-58), by Daris to the gatekeeper (ll.607-818), and by the gatekeeper to Clarice (ll.850-68). In the meantime Floris has used three disguises: that of a merchant (l.370), that of an engineer or builder (ll.748-50), and that of a 'flower' in a basket of flowers (l.854). Rather than tracing 'magic' or 'fertility' or other symbolic origins for the number three, it is helpful to realize that in children's games and in play between grown-up and child such generally agreed numbers—usually three or a hundred—serve as suspense-building devices. Whether or not the number three has connotations of perfect harmony, the repetition certainly has a formal function. On the symbolic level it may point to integrity to be gained, but as a formal pattern it is also a suspense-building device, in the same way that, later on, the introduction of the Emir's chamberlain and the calling in of the barons near the end are suspense-building devices.

Because it is not the individual characters but the whole action that represents human experience in this type of story, the setting and the 'stage properties' must also be considered as part of the experience.

Fl & Bl appears to progress by means of situations and objects of an archetypal nature. The archetypal situations of a young lover's conflicts with father and rivals and his experience with women and guides have been sketched above.[2] Of archetypal 'props' the most outstanding are the tomb, the ring, the precious stones, the chalices or cups, and the flowers. In this formal type of story these 'props' are to be read as symbolic agents in the total experience.

The recurrent symbols marking the progress of *Fl & Bl* are the cup and the ring. It is typical of this story that the progress should be marked by female symbols rather than male ones such as swords and lances. There is no mention of weapons, as there is no fighting, chivalric or otherwise. The love idealism portrayed in *Fl & Bl* concentrates on the adolescent hero's quest for integration of the feminine aspects of life, excluding the simultaneous development of the masculine aspects.

The cup appears in two forms. The cup that was given in payment for Blauncheflour (ll.161-82) is central. Instead of the girl herself, a symbol of her remains behind. Floris would not be 'alive' without her presence, even if only in a symbolic form. Therefore, when he sets out to be reunited with Blauncheflour, that *ilke self*

---

[2] For a further discussion along Jungian lines, see Reiss, 1971:339-50.

coupe (1.373: 'very same cup') is given to him by his father because
Herewiþ þou may þat swete þing / Wynne (ll.376-7: 'with this you
can win back that sweet girl'). The cup points out the purpose of
Floris' quest and does turn out to be the key that opens the gate to the
girl. It is the right equipment to gain admittance, and therefore convinces the gatekeeper (ll.781-822).

So, by staying behind, the cup shows the hero what he must go
in search of if he is to be re-integrated. As long as that has not been
achieved, Floris is not really 'alive', which is illustrated by the fact
that he goes without food because he misses her (ll.129-30; 417-18;
493-4; 577-83). Characteristically, when he receives information
about Blauncheflour, he rewards his guides with cups (ll.444-8; 517-
22). These other cups emphasize the role of the first cup as pointer:
Floris can symbolically give his cup away in exchange for directions
towards Blauncheflour. When he comes to her actual gatekeeper, he
does so literally.

The ring, which in psychology as in alchemy not only symbolizes the female but also truth (since it has neither beginning nor
end), operates on both these symbolic levels. When Floris has
reached the point when he can set out to win his love, it is given to
him—typically—by his mother.

> Haue nou, sone, here þis ring;
> While þou hit hast, doute þe no þing,
> Ne fir þe brenne, ne drenchen in se,
> Ne iren ne stel schal derie þe;
> And be hit erli and be hit late,
> To þi wille þou schalt haue whate.   (391-6)

(Now, my sone, take this ring. Be not afraid of anything as long as
you possess it: no fire shall burn you, you shall not drown in the
sea. Neither iron nor steel shall harm you. And whether early or
late, you shall have the wherewithal to satisfy your wants.)

This incantation-like speech indicates that now, when he has shown
himself independent enough to set out, he can wear this ring which,
like the cup, adds the feminine aspect to his male personality, thus
making him whole. And with that integrity he shall be safe against
the elements, which are hostile to him as long as he has not achieved
integration, as his mother's words imply: against the fire, the water
and the iron that can kill him. And the sustaining earth shall not fail
him.

Parallel to this, another ring is given to Floris by his last host on the way, to be given to Daris (ll.555-8). This ring also protects him, here from the effects of being a stranger, and it serves to identify him to his next and most essential guide. This ring tells Daris the truth about Floris the lover. And telling the truth about Floris and Blauncheflour is also what the first ring ultimately does (ll.1149ff). Its protective power is again hinted at: *Þou ne schalt nowt die whiles hit is þin* (l.1152: 'you shall not die as long as it is yours'). But its protective effect is shown to consist in its showing the truth of the great—because essential—love between the two. It is not its magic but its symbolism that is effective. It is the fact that both insist on the other's wearing it, sacrificing their own lives for the sake of the other, that convinces the Emir that this is a true love that he must not destroy.

The quest for Blauncheflour is a quest from death to life. Their union is life in social terms; their separation is death, as the tomb scene emphasizes. At Blauncheflour's supposed tomb Floris realizes that for him by himself there is no life. So he decides to commit suicide (ll.301-12). This scene illustrates that parental restraint, when pushed to the absolute, is death for the child. The child must be able to get out on its own, in order to achieve an identity and a place of its own in the whole. Floris' identity threatens to be killed until, as I said above, his mother gives life to him again by preventing his suicide.

Also Floris' swooning on various occasions suggests that apparently insuperable obstacles to his reunion mean for him the loss of his identity—here symbolized as consciousness. He swoons for the first time when he hears from her mother that Blauncheflour is dead (l.246), and three times, so more absolutely, when he is reading the inscription on her tomb (l.267). And he is once more to swoon three times when he has heard how absolutely inaccessible Blauncheflour is in the Emir's power.

Having progressed 'through' the tomb, Floris begins to show— temporary—signs of independence: *Now, moder, y þink þat y leve may* (l.341: 'Mother, I believe that I can leave now'). And he even takes command: *"Leue fader," he seide, "y telle þe / Al þat þou shalt fynde me"* (l.355-6: '"Dear father," he said, "I shall name you all that you must provide me with"'). But his initiation to life is by no means complete. He has so far only been initiated into the quest stage. His approach to union is marked by obstacles, as if it consists of so many stages. Each of these obstacles is of a kind that could have

symbolic power, but this does not appear to be worked out in this
rendering of the tale. The first obstacle after the tomb is water, the
salte flod that he must cross (1.455). It marks the beginning of the
Babylon stage. The second obstacle is a bridge (ll. 549-52), at the
end of which he shall find his most essential guide Daris. This bridge
he 'achieves' by means of the above-mentioned second ring. Between
his guide and his goal is the third obstacle, the city-wall of Babylon
and its defending knights (ll.608-34). And ultimately there is the
tower with its eunuchs and gatekeeper (ll.635-78).

    With the tower in Babylon the obstacles do acquire symbolic
power: *And in þe bourh, amide periȝt / Þer stant a riche tour, I þe
aplyȝt* (ll.635-6: 'and in the city, right in the middle, there stands a
rich tower, I assure you'). The tower in its setting of Babylon or the
orchard almost suggests a *mandala*: it possesses a number of the perennial symbols of the achievement of inner wholeness. It is crowned
with a sun-like jewel (ll. 655-60) and it is presented as a place of
bliss:

> So wel were þat ilke man
> Þat miȝte wonen in þat an,
> Nou þourt him neuere, ful iwis,
> Willen after more blisse.   (663-6)

(Any man who would be able to live in it would be fortunate to such
a degree that he need not, indeed, ever wish for greater happiness.)

    The description of the Emir's orchard adds to the symbolic
power of the setting in which Blaunchefloūr is found. The description of Paradise in the *Book of Genesis*, and most especially in Mil-
ton's *Paradise Lost*, Book IV, as also the description of the Garden in
the *Roman de la Rose*, show that a setting of the Tree of Love and/or
a Tree of Life and a fountain and flowers, birds and precious stones
is felt to be the appropriate one for love and integrity. The Emir's
locus amoenus likewise has birds (1.691), precious stones (ll.693-6
and 701-3), a well from Paradise (ll.697-700), a Tree of Love (ll.
721-3) and flowers (ll.724-6).

    In *Fl & Bl* it is, and at the same time is not, the place of re-
union of the lovers. Tower and orchard suggest that this is the final
place where the quest finds its fulfilment. The object of the quest,
Blaunchefloūr, is there in the appropriate setting for what she is for
Floris. That this 'enemy territory' presents itself primarily, in its

imagery, as the place of achievement of the desired object, must be understood in the light of the fact that in this type of story every element is to be seen in relation to the protagonist. Inner wholeness is to be achieved there, so the setting suggests. But the final achievement contains in itself also the final test.The place constitutes, at the same time, a major danger from which Floris must rescue Blaunche-flour and himself: a paradise—symbol of social achievement—manipulated by the false values of the Emir, whose abominable fertility-cult of mating for the season is a perversion of the perfect love that the romance seeks: a fully integrated social ideal, based on loyalty instead of manipulation and on love instead of mere pleasure.

But Floris is not yet ready to achieve this rescue. First he must pass the Cerberus-gatekeeper into the underworld of a symbolic death, to rise to life again in his proper form in the basket of flowers. The gatekeeper first appears as another peacock-rival or obstacle to Floris' achievement of love, prefiguring one aspect of the Emir (ll.679-80), but in the detailed instructions that follow he is presented as a Cerberus controlling the entrance to the Paradise of Blaunche-flour's setting. Like the porter to the Underworld of Greek mythology he is said to rob the applicant of his possessions: *He wille him bope bete and reue* (l.678: 'he will beat as well as rob him'). He is wary of people who are just curious:

> Wel sone he wil come to þe
> And aske what mister man þou be
> And ber vpon þe felonie,
> And saie þou art comen þe tour aspie. (753-6)
> (translation: see p.57)

Serious applicants for entrance he submits to the test of the game of chess, by which they must pay for his services in conducting them in.

The game of chess (ll.764-814) is traditionally an initiation through symbolic death and rebirth. Floris' boyish dependence on others will have to die, so that he shall be reborn as a man able to play his own game. The gatekeeper shall not be his guide, but his servant. How much effort this development takes, what price Floris must pay, is indicated by the three stages that the game takes, with doubled and tripled stakes and finally by the sacrifice of the cup itself which symbolizes Floris' life, as I have argued above.

After this Cerberus' assistance—the first integration or loyalty—has been secured by Floris' symbolic death, the seed of the new

hero is buried in the coffin of the basket, from which the flower
Floris will resurrect. Dramatizing the continual risk to which the
ideal is exposed, he is carried to the 'wrong' place, so that his resurrection might yet prove death, acted out as Floris' diving back into
the basket again (ll.861-78). But the girl Clarice, to whose room he
has been carrried, 'revives' him, thus prefiguring an aspect of
Blauncheflour. She shows a further integration, now of a woman's
capacity for fellow-feeling, healing and tender care:

> 'Ne doute ȝou nammore wiþalle
> Þan to miself hit hadde bifalle.
> Wite ȝe wel witerli
> Þat hele ich wille ȝoure boþer druri.'
> To on bedde ȝhe haþ hem ibrowt
> Þat was of silk and sendal wrout.
> Þai sette hem þere wel softe adoun,
> And Clarice drowȝ þe courtyn roun.   (953-60)

('Be no more afraid in this matter than if it had happened to me. You
may rest assured that I will keep the love between the two of you a
secret.' She took them to a bed that was made with silk and sendal.
They lay down in it very comfortably and Clarice drew the curtain
round them.)

Now Floris and Blauncheflour are finally reunited, but their
quest has not yet come to an end. Their place in the whole of society
they still have to win. The parental and jealous rival figure of the
Emir demands final proof of their love. A last initiation awaits them.
Their enclosure in a dungeon (l.1088) symbolizes that they must die
again, now together. But they only achieve their ultimate initiation
by voluntarily accepting literal death, the one sacrificing himself or
herself for the other. This scene of their mutually taking the blame
and of the insistent exchanging of the protective ring (ll.1135-82),
followed by their taking each other's place under the Emir's sword
(ll.1193-1230), reveals their full beauty, the glory of their true love,
for all to see.

In *Fl & Bl*, then, we have indulged the fancy and we have heard of
love, in that order. How perennial this experience is, every lover of
Mozart's *The Magic Flute* will recognize. The Middle English *Fl &
Bl* has rendered the experiences simply and briskly. The rich archetypal suggestiveness does not clog the pure and direct manner of the

narrative. What Atkins referred to as a "good tale" turns out to be a well-structured tale: without the support of any extensive discussion or moral, the carefully handled formal and symbolic patterns bring out the significance of the tale in the most immediate manner.

REFERENCES

Atkins, J.W.H. (1907). Metrical Romances, 1200-1500. II. In: *The Cambridge History of English Literature*. Ed. A.W. Ward and A.R. Waller. Vol. I. Cambridge: C.U.P. 301-19.
Reiss, E. (1971). Symbolic Detail in Medieval Narrative: *Floris and Blancheflour*. *Papers in Language and Literature* 7. 339-50.
Stevens, J. (1973). *Medieval Romance: Themes and Approaches*. London: Hutchinson.
Taylor, A.B. (ed.) (1927). *Floris and Blauncheflour: A Middle English Romance. Edited from the Trentham and Auchinleck MSS*. Oxford: O.U.P.

DAME SIRITH AND DE CLERICO ET PUELLA

KEITH BUSBY
(University of Oklahoma)

A good deal of Middle English literature is derived either directly or indirectly from Old French. Genres that make their first appearance on the continent (or in England in French-speaking circles) are later taken over by authors writing in English. The French influence on Middle English literature is almost incalculable, as it is both pervasive and persistent, and assumes many forms. The most evident of these forms is, of course, the translation from French into English, but instances of literal translation from one language into another are rare in the Middle Ages in general. Whilst there are many cases of what look like translations, closer examination reveals that they are actually adaptations: English poets working with a French text in front of them tailor it to fit the tastes and requirements of a new and different audience.

Whilst the narrative line of, say, Chrétien de Troyes's Arthurian romance *Yvain* (*Le Chevalier au Lion*) remains intact in the adaptation, the essence of the poem does not. Chrétien's original aristocratic audience appreciated the finer points of courtly, chivalric, and amorous behaviour, and took great pleasure in listening to detailed and often rhetorical analysis of sentiment; the Middle English *Ywain and Gawain*, on the other hand, seems to have been destined for a public of fourteenth-century *nouveaux riches* who did not apparently appreciate this aspect of Chrétien's poem, and the English version is consequently transformed from a courtly romance into a fast-moving story of adventure. Another type of work that shows the profound influence of French literature on English is original English works written with a detailed knowledge of French texts and constituting in some ways responses to them. Staying with Arthurian romance for the moment, the best example is probably *Sir Gawain and the Green Knight*, a poem for which no French model exists, but which shows indisputable knowledge (and understanding) of the French tradition. Although inconceivable without the French Gauvain, the English Gawain is very English indeed. On a more general level, themes, modes, images, styles of writing that developed first in French are taken up later and anglicized. Without the model of French, English medieval literature would have been very different.

It may seem rather odd to have started this chapter, which deals with *Dame Sirith* and *De Clerico et Puella*, by mentioning two Arthurian romances, which are at first sight unrelated to our texts. However, whereas Middle English literature of the fourteenth century, generally speaking, reflects in its own way the constitution of the corpus of French, there are some types of literature that are notable for their scarcity in Middle English, although they abound in French. One of these is the *fabliau*, of which *Dame Sirith* is the only undisputed example outside of Chaucer's works; whilst *De Clerico* cannot be called a *fabliau* proper, it is clearly related to the genre (I shall return to this in my brief discussion of the poem towards the end of this paper). In my opinion, the absence of *fabliaux* in Middle English is intimately linked to both the nature of romance and the language situation in the British Isles in the Middle Ages.

First, however, a word about *fabliaux* in general. The word *fabliau* is a Picard (North-Eastern) dialect form of *fableau* (also attested), derived from Latin *fabulellum*, a diminutive of *fabula*. Without going into the detailed historical semantics of these words, the Old French word *fableau/fabliau* means literally 'little story, little fiction'. Scholars use the Picard form to designate the genre because it seems to have flourished in North-Eastern France more than in other regions, and this in the thirteenth and fourteenth centuries. There have been many attempts to define the *fabliau*, most of them unsatisfactory in one way or another, and indeed, the matter is one of the most notorious problems of French literary scholarship. The attempts clearly fail because the poems regarded as *fabliaux* are many and varied, and resist strict categorisation. Moreover, the modern mania for definitions almost certainly does not correspond to the medieval view of literature. In fact, the only "definition" that has won currency in scholarly circles is an extremely loose one formulated by the great French scholar Joseph Bédier as early as 1894: "les fabliaux sont des contes à rire en vers" ('the fabliaux are comic tales in verse'). The obvious reservations that have to be made about this phrase are that there are other comic tales in verse not generally regarded as *fabliaux* and that some poems generally accepted to be *fabliaux* are not very humorous, at least not to our eyes. Rather than become involved here in the hornet's nest of genre-definitions and related problems, I shall give a brief *description*, not *definition*, of the *fabliaux*.

The *fabliaux* vary in length from about fifty to over one thousand lines and are almost without exception written in octosyllabic rhyming couplets. They treat a wide variety of subjects, but are frequently—but not exclusively—concerned with what we sometimes call "low" life. The *fabliaux* are usually set in a rural or urban (but not normally aristocratic) setting, and the characters are peasants, merchants, their wives, and priests or monks; the nobility appear only infrequently, but their appearance is not insignificant. In *fabliaux*, we may see the parish priest making love with the baker's wife and being castrated as punishment; we may see examples of native peasant cunning, which nearly all involve practical jokes; sex, food, and excrement also feature widely in the *fabliaux*, and there are few subjects that are taboo. Common to most of the *fabliaux* is the idea of ruse and deception, and the plot of many of them revolves around some form of trick. In keeping with the setting and subject-matter, the style of the *fabliaux* is frequently less courtly than, say, that of the romance, but there are notable exceptions.

It is not difficult to understand, in the light of this brief description, why the *fabliaux* were for many years considered to be the bourgeois or peasant counterpart to courtly literature. After all, the subjects are usually far from courtly, and much closer to the world of the bourgeoisie and peasantry than to that of the aristocracy. Yet, when the matter is considered logically, considerable problems arise. Are merchants and peasants likely to enjoy literature in which their peers without exception are made to look foolish? How do we explain the presence of *fabliaux* in the same manuscripts as religious poems, romances, and other forms of courtly literature? We are, of course, dealing with what is probably the most difficult of all issues that confront the medieval literary scholar, that of the intended audience of the literature.

The question of the audience of *fabliaux* used until fairly recently to be discussed in terms of clear-cut social categories: either they were meant for the bourgeoisie (Bédier's thesis) or they were intended for the aristocracy (Per Nykrog's thesis of 1957). Whilst Bédier's assumption was based on the subject-matter (non-courtly for a non-courtly audience), Nykrog's took as its point of departure the presence of parody. There is a good deal of parody in the *fabliaux*, notably of courtly literature, and parody is ineffective unless the audience appreciates what is being parodied. *Ergo*, since the *fabliaux* parody courtly literature, they must share the same audience. There can be no denying the validity of this thesis: some *fabliaux* are even built up of themes and narrative elements proper to the courtly romance; some contain specific allusions to, even quotations from, courtly texts.

It hardly needs to be said that the truth is more complicated, and that the one theory does not necessarily exclude the other, for whilst courtly literature may, initially at least, have been intended exclusively for the nobility, there is no reason to believe that the *fabliaux* were as socially confined as romance. Indeed, their nature is such that they must have appealed to many different kinds of medieval people. In what is probably the most sophisticated and tolerant discussion to date of *fabliaux* audiences, Jean Rychner has shown how different versions of the same poem can be explained as adaptations for audiences with a different make-up. Thus, a *fabliau* with elements of courtly parody may be rewritten for a non-courtly audience, the courtly allusions, etc., being omitted since they would not be appreciated. The process may also take place in the other direction. On the other hand, the non-courtly audience could have appreciated the basic humour of a tale as it was, even though the parody was beyond them, and there was nothing to stop a sophisticated courtly audience having a belly-laugh at a poem which contained no courtly parody. We are probably much nearer the truth if we think of a heterogeneous audience containing people from all walks of life, rather than a homogeneous one made up of *either* the aristocracy *or* the bourgeoisie *and/or* the peasantry.

By and large, it does not seem to me that there is any real reason for not actually considering the *fabliaux* as part and parcel of courtly literature, particularly in view of their manuscript context mentioned above. In this respect, then, and by virtue of their relationship to the kind of literature they parody, the *fabliaux* partly owe their existence to romance, upon which they offer a kind of down-to-earth commentary. This can be seen as one of the reasons for the curious lack of *fabliaux* in Middle English, for the kind of elements of courtly literature that are parodied (the love interest, the finer points of courtly and chivalric behaviour, etc.) are generally the aspects that receive less attention in Middle English romance as a whole. Thus, since the object of the parody does not exist in English romance, one of the *raisons d' être* of the French *fabliau* is not operative in the English situation.

The other major reason for the paucity of *fabliaux* in English has to do with linguistic conditions. For a good part of the Middle Ages, French was the language of the majority of the aristocracy in England, and thus of literature. The consequence is that most Old French literature was comprehensible to English audiences for the twelfth and thirteenth centuries and much of the fourteenth. The French *fabliaux* almost certainly circulated in England, and indeed, a number of them are written in Anglo-Norman, the insular dialect of French spoken and written by the Norman rulers of England. It is therefore not necessary to speak of the English *fabliaux* as forming part of a vast "lost literature of medieval England", or to speculate that the English did not share the *esprit gaulois* of the French and their taste for the scurrilous and bawdy. It is fair to conclude that there was little need for *fabliaux* in Middle English for most of the Middle Ages, as they were regarded as a type of poem better suited to expression in French. Similar arguments can be brought to bear as an explanation for the equally curious lack of animal epic (*Roman de Renart*) or animal fable in Middle English, represented outside of Chaucer's works only by *The Fox and the Wolf* (found in the same manuscript as *Dame Sirith*).

As for Chaucer, he is, as usual, a remarkable exception to the rule. *The Canterbury Tales* contain a number of *fabliaux* (the most celebrated of which are no doubt *The Miller's Tale* and *The Reeve's Tale*) and an animal fable (*The Nun's Priest's Tale*). It has been suggested that one of Chaucer's aims in *The Canterbury Tales* was to give a survey of the different types of narrative genre current in his time. Since Chaucer is thoroughly Gallicised (but in a very English way), it is not surprising to find his narrative universe containing examples of the *fabliau* and the animal fable, for they also respond to the more courtly tales in the collection. *The Miller's Tale* is both a general and a specific reaction to *The Knight's Tale*: it is *fabliau* responding to romance; it is told by the drunken miller in an attempt to "quite" the Knight; it is also concerned with the rivalry of two men for one woman ..., etc. *The Miller's Tale* exploits the potential of the *fabliaux* as no French poem does, and *The Nun's Priest's Tale*, whilst clearly an animal fable, exceeds its French models, with the possible exception of *Isopet*, by exploring in the most absurd fashion the theme of the power of rhetoric.

Dame Sirith and the Weeping Bitch is thus something of an oddity in Middle English, and perhaps all the more interesting because of that.

I have already mentioned that it is contained in the same manuscript as *The Fox and the Wolf*, and this is probably not a coincidence. MS. Digby 86 of the Bodleian Library in Oxford is an anthology of pieces in verse and prose in Middle English, Anglo-Norman, and Latin. There are a number of manuscripts like it, the most famous of which is probably the precious MS. Harley 2253 of the British Library, a comparable but not identical collection. The compiler of Digby 86, a relatively early manuscript, shows signs of a desire to be fashionable, and the presence of the *fabliau* of *Dame Sirith* and the animal fable of *The Fox and the Wolf* can therefore be attributed to this desire. In addition, he also seems to have had a predilection for particularly scurrilous poetry, as he has also included the Anglo-Norman *Lai du Cor* (a chastity-test that takes place at Arthur's court) and one of the most disgusting French *fabliaux*, *Les Quatre Souhaits Saint Martin*, scarcely repeatable even in summary.

This is not the place to explore in detail the analogues to *Dame Sirith* and to discuss the relationships between them. Suffice it to say here that there are plenty of similar stories, not only in the corpus of French *fabliaux*, but also in Oriental story collections. This need not astonish us, for the nature of the *fabliau* plot in general is such that folklorists can provide us with interesting material for comparison. We should not, however, make the mistake of regarding *fabliaux* as traditional folktale, for some of them are very sophisticated literary productions, despite their frequently scurrilous subject-matter.

The Anglo-Norman heading in the manuscript suggests what kind of a poem *Dame Sirith* is: it is a *fablel* (a variant of *fabliau*) concerned with the *cointise* of Dame Sirith. *Cointise* is a word with many meanings in Old French, but here it clearly indicates something like "cleverness, ingenuity", leading the audience to believe that this is the main subject of the poem. Indeed, after we have read or listened to *Dame Sirith*, what remains in our mind is not the love of Willikin for Margery, but the trick by means of which Dame Sirith brings about their union.

The poem opens in a traditional "minstrel" manner, with an announcement of the source (ll.1-2) and then the subject (ll.3-15). It is therefore already evident that the poem is going to be concerned with the lover's attempts to win the lady. The style of the opening is also typical of certain other Middle English poems, with ll.4-6 in particular recalling the romance tradition by virtue of their use of short alliterative formulae. The social setting of the poem is also indicated by the mention of the husband's profession (l.18); he is a merchant, so this is to be no poem of courtly love between knights and ladies. Still the alliterative formulae pile up (ll.21, 23).

Starting with l.25, the poem makes full use of dialogue, even to the extent of making itself susceptible of performance; it is not difficult to imagine how a talented *jongleur* or minstrel could have exploited the dialogue, changing voices (and possibly even hats) as the speech alternated from one character to another. The merchant's wife is the object of the as yet unnamed protagonist's affections, as had already been indicated in l.20. In the light of his imminent amorous confession, her offer to do anything he desires (ll.29-36) acquires in retrospect an ironic tinge, and is obviously not meant by her to be taken absolutely literally. The direct and sudden declaration of love that follows (ll.67 ff.) is in itself interesting: had this been a courtly poem, the characters would no doubt have been shown suffering torments of love and analysing their sentiments in great rhetorical detail before stammering out a bashful declaration. Whilst the poet had said in l.9 that the lover *heuede wrong* (probably 'suffered anguish or pain', rather than 'committed a sin'), there is not much timidity about him. The declaration is preceded by a repeated statement of a "courtly" desire not to offend her in any way (ll.38-9, 41-2). The whole scene itself invites comparison with Nicholas's first approach to Alison in Chaucer's *The Miller's Tale*.

The courtly influence becomes steadily more apparent in the lady's reply to the as yet unspecified request: *houncurteis* (l.46) and *vilte* (l.47) are both words of French origin and belong to romance and lyric poetry. The humour of this passage lies, as I have suggested, in her suggestion that she will accede to his request, providing she does not incur shame; the eventual granting or denial of her love she makes dependent on his eloquence and persuasiveness (ll.52-3). Furthermore, her assurance that she will not blame him for whatever he might say seems to relieve him of any tension and enables him to express himself freely. He has won himself a fair hearing and so cannot grumble (ll.58-60). Interestingly, he calls the lady's response to his request *hende* (l.61), which is one of the Middle English words used alongside *curteis* and *fre* (cf. l.34) to denote 'courteous' or 'courtly'.

The lover now makes his true confession (ll.66 ff.): he has loved her for many years, but was afraid to visit her while her husband was in town. The absence of the husband to visit the fair in Boston is at the same time a narrative device common in *fabliaux* (which makes the lover's visit possible) and a method of locating the

action in a typically provincial setting (French *fabliaux* are rarely set
in Paris, but rather in Normandy, Abbeville, Arras, etc.). The im-
plied possessiveness (ll.70-73, 82-4) of the husband also marks him
as a *mari jaloux*, possibly even a *senex amans* ('old lover'), one of
the stereotypes not only of the *fabliaux* but also of such courtly
literature as the *Lais* of Marie de France or a good proportion of the
courtly lyric in both Provençal and French. The lover's speech
switches constantly in tone from the non-courtly (the invitation to
bed, your husband has gone to Boston, etc.) to the courtly (do not be
offended, you speak courteously, etc.), and ll.85-7 are the words and
sentiment of the typical courtly lover: "Lady, if it is your will, I will
love you secretly and silently." Secrecy is indeed one of the notable
characteristics of that variety of love that critics have often called, in
the wake of Gaston Paris and C.S. Lewis, *amour courtois* or *courtly
love*, and which I have myself alluded to earlier. Whilst we must
bear in mind that courtly love is an invention of modern scholars and
that we should not expect to find the "classic" variety (eventual adultery between beseeching lover and pitiless lady of higher social class,
secrecry, suffering, refined analysis of sentiment, etc.) in every or
even any single text, it is still a handy concept if used cautiously.
    The lady's reaction to this confession is disappointing, espe-
cially in the light of her earlier hint of readiness to oblige: she
indignantly invokes the holy sacrament of marriage, the duty of wife
to husband (*louerd* and *spouse*, l.91), and the strength of the love
between them. Nor does she wish to soil her reputation as an honest
woman; the indignant and proper tone of the rebuke is vitiated somewhat by l.102, where she specifies precisely where she will not *don
selk falsete*. The lover's disappointment is evident, but he does not
give up hope, reminding her once more of her *curteisi* (l.110), and
hoping that God will change her mind (just as she had earlier called
on Him whilst expressing the opposite sentiment). The lady's next
speech is another mixture of the courtly and the non-courtly. She
begins by asking whether he takes her for a fool, and then questions
his sanity in no uncertain terms (ll.115-17). The description of her
husband (ll.119-20) is couched in the purest courtly language (*curteis, hende, pris* [another French word]), and she once more stresses
her own wifely virtue and honour (ll.121-6). Again, the lover's reaction is traditional and courtly: *Swete lemmon* (l.127) is the standard
mode of address of lover to lady in Middle English love poetry;
vilani (l.128) is another French word belonging to the vocabulary of
love; the importance of the secrecy of the love is repeated (l.130);

won ('happiness', 1.132) seems to be the equivalent of the *joi* of Troubadour lyric poetry, which often stands for the successful culmination of the lover's suit in sexual and spiritual union.

The lover's departure is again characteristic: the lady is pitiless, even sarcastic (ll.134-5), in her rejection, bringing very much to mind the *Belle Dame sans Merci* of courtly lyric and romance. And the lover, repeating helplessly the lady's remark about wasting his time and effort (ll.134, 140-41), and indulging in self-pity but not giving up hope (for a courtly lover never does), leaves with another appeal to Heaven to make his beloved change her mind.

This constitutes the end of the first section of the narrative, and leads into the lover's first meeting with the go-between, Dame Sirith. The go-between is a common figure in literature in general, and particularly common in the *fabliaux* (for obvious reasons), whilst not altogether absent from romance (one thinks notably of the servant-girl Lunete in Chrétien de Troyes's *Yvain*). Although the lover is *drerimod* (1.149) and generally depressed, he is not entirely at his wit's end, retaining a fair level of self-composure, enough in any case to offer Dame Sirith (note that she is also, ironically, called *hende* in 1.154) money in return for her services. In a sense, the encounter between the lover and Dame Sirith is a structural variation on his meeting with the lady (now revealed as *Margeri*, 1.177). He requests her for help, without specifying its precise nature (ll.161-6); she expresses willingness to co-operate and asks for further details (ll.167-72); in his reply he assumes once more the role and tone of the rebuffed courtly lover, even going so far as to suggest that he may commit suicide unless the lady changes her mind (ll.173-84). Dame Sirith's secondary response is, like the lady's, indignant, and she appeals to God, claiming that acceding to his request would entail loss of virtue and would bring shame on herself. In fact, her greatest concern is to rid herself of the suspicion of witchcraft (certainly not hinted at in the text). The combination of the lover's reassurance and the offer of money and clothing begins to change her mind.

Dame Sirith is also concerned that her client (now called *Wilekin*, 1.229) really does love Margery (ll.229-31), and especially that he intends to keep the affair secret, for otherwise she runs the risk of being accused of complicity in an immoral act and actually being taken to court (1.244). Here, an aspect of the traditional courtly love affair, the secrecy, is presented in what is effectively another mode: until now, it had been put only by Willikin as *dernelike* (1.86) and *derne loue* (1.130), both conventional phrases; now the secrecy is important for practical reasons to an old woman afraid of legal prosecution. With Willikin's repeated assurance of his good intentions, the scene is now set for Dame Sirith's contribution, and the audience now turn their attention to exactly how this old lady with a reputation for cunning is going to persuade Margery to grant her favours to Willikin. There is little doubt at this point that Willikin will succeed: from a narrative point of view, the problem and situation are evident, and all the ingredients necessary for the resolution are present. We are therefore now concerned with *how*, not *whether*, things will work out.

It is true that Dame Sirith herself almost suggests that she is about to practice some form of magic in order to achieve her ends (ll.264-6, 276-8), but Willikin's offer of twenty pounds for her trouble reduces the affair to a more mercenary level. The poet maintains suspense, for even after Dame Sirith's saying she will give pepper, mustard and vinegar to the dog (ll.279-81), and Willikin's sceptical, not to say incomprehending, reaction, the audience is still in the dark as to exactly what her plans are. We know no more than Willikin at this point: simply that she will *make a lesing* (l.282) of some kind. Dame Sirith also refers to the ruse she is planning as a *gin* (l.289), derived from Old French *engin*, one of the words commonly used to describe a trick in the *fabliaux*. Willikin is to wait until Dame Sirith returns from her visit to Margery.

The suspense is kept up as Dame Sirith goes to Margery's house and laments loudly about her pitiable state (ll.297-314). Margery falls for the deception, invites her in and offers to feed her (ll.315-30). Note the narrator's comment on Dame Sirith, *Christ awarie hire lif!* (l.332: 'May Christ damn her way of life!'), which is tantamount to approval of whatever it is she is about to do. The old woman then begins a tale about her married daughter being courted by a clerk (ll.338 ff.) which bears a not entirely coincidental relationship to the story of Willikin's frustrated courtship of Margery. It is at this point, when we see the parallel between the two tales, that we begin to get some intimation of what she is up to, especially when she says that the clerk in love with her daughter has turned her into a bitch because she did not return his love. Her pointing to the dog, weeping, of course, because of the pepper, mustard and vinegar, is the narrative equivalent of the conjuror's pulling a rabbit out of the hat (ll.335ff). From the particular case of her daughter, she draws a general conclusion (ll.361-4) which has the desired effect on Margery, now terrified that Willikin will bewitch her, too (ll.365-70).

Dame Sirith's *gin* has worked, to Willikin's benefit, we may now confidently assume, and doubly to her own, for not only does she stand to receive Willikin's money but Margery's gifts as well (ll.388-90). *Dame Sirith* now ends swiftly and predictably, for once the old woman's ingenuity has been revealed and admired, the poet realises as a good storyteller that there is little point in prolonging his tale. Willikin is about to achieve his desire, though not because Margery has changed her feelings towards him, despite her apparent recapitulation in ll.425-32. There is a cynical contrast between Margery's motivation (fear of being turned into a dog) and the terms in which she offers herself to Willikin, which are those of the courtly lover. This type of love-language we have noticed earlier in the poem, but this is really the first time it has been used by Margery. Dame Sirith's own final speech, the last of the poem as a whole, is equally cynical. It is clear, first of all, exactly what love means to her (ll.440-41) and exactly what she expects Willikin to get up to as soon as she has left; secondly, her parting words, addressed to the audience as much as the other characters, amount to a kind of professional statement on her own behalf and that of other go-betweens.

The *Interludium de Clerico et Puella* is a slighter piece than *Dame Sirith*. It is important, however, for the history of English drama, although it is probably something of an exaggeration to call it the oldest secular play extant in English. In fact, like *Dame Sirith*, it may well have been intended for recitation by a single *jongleur* or minstrel rather than for a "theatrical" performance by a number of actors. Its treatment of basically the same theme as *Dame Sirith* is more economical and arguably more immediate and dramatic. Because of its brevity, its author does not have the time to employ the stylistic and narrative devices that make *Dame Sirith* what it is, but there are remarkable resemblances between the two poems. These can be found not only on the plot level (it is likely that *De Clerico* would have been a complete analogue to *Dame Sirith*, had it been preserved fully), but also on the verbal and stylistic (some of these are given by Bennett and Smithers, p.372). Whilst the influence of the courtly style is less evident in *De Clerico*, it is not entirely lacking (cf. the clerk's lament in ll.17-26, and the use of romance loanwords such as *clerc fayllard* [1.8], *trua* [1.35], *cunsayle* [1.54]). However, given the nature of both pieces and their relationship to the *fabliau* tradition, there seems little point in attempting to establish a direct link between the two: while we cannot rule out the possibility that the one is an abbreviated or expanded version of the other, it is more likely that they are simply two out of many versions of the story that may have once existed. In its verse-form, *De Clerico* is closer than most of *Dame Sirith* to the Old French *fabliau*: whilst it is not written in octosyllabic couplets, *De Clerico* shows rhyming couplets with four beats which approximate to the French form. Scholars have yet to provide a satisfactory explanation for the alternating verse patterns in *Dame Sirith*.

Dame Sirith and *De Clerico et Puella* prove, if proof were required, that English poetry before Chaucer is not lacking in humour. One of the major issues of *fabliau* scholarship used to be that of whether the genre was a moral one or not, for it was thought that the idea of literature for entertainment did not really exist in the Middle Ages. Medieval literature, of course, was allowed some entertainment value by earlier scholars, but it was also required to instruct at the same time (*prodesse et delectare*, 'to instruct and delight' is a common phrase in medieval poetics). Not all critics now accept this dictum. After all, the moral, if there is one, of *Dame Sirith* and *De Clerico et Puella*, is not only cynical, but meagre and rather banal. Like a good deal of medieval literature, however, these two pieces are still worth reading simply because they are good stories well told.

REFERENCES

(In addition to those given in J.A.W. Bennett and G.V. Smithers, eds., *Early Middle English Verse and Prose*, Oxford: O.U.P., 2nd ed., 1968. (1st ed., 1966.))

Bédier, J (1894). *Les Fabliaux*. Paris: Champion. (6th ed., 1969.)
*Busby, K. (1982). Conspicuous by its Absence: the English Fabliau. *Dutch Quarterly Review* 12. 30-41.
Duval, J., and R. Eichmann (tr.) (1982). *Cuckolds, Clerics, and Countrymen.* ? [Translations into English of a selection of Old French Fabliaux.] · Fayetteville, AR: University of Arkansas Press.
Muscatine, C. (1986). *The Old French Fabliaux*. New Haven, CT: Yale U.P.
Nykrog, P. (1957). *Les Fabliaux*. Geneva: Droz.
Rychner, J. (1960). *Contribution à l'étude des fabliaux*. 2 vols. Geneva: Droz.

THE FOX AND THE WOLF
A STUDY IN MEDIEVAL IRONY

WIM TIGGES
(University of Leiden)

After critical neglect for more than half a century, the tale of *The Fox and the Wolf* has more recently inspired several scholars to a renewed approach to its obvious merits; 'obvious' because as H. Bergner (1973: 268) has remarked, the tale is included in all the important anthologies of Middle English literature. Bergner was responding to two studies in which its satirical aspects are discussed: Bercovitch (1966) and Von Kreisler (1970). These three articles, the first to adopt an analytical rather than a contextual approach, form the basis of the present study. I do not intend, therefore, to summarize the early scholarship, which has been aptly presented by Bergner in particular[1], nor to rehearse the history of the treatment of the theme of *The Fox and the Wolf* (henceforth *FW*), which is most conveniently summed up by G.V. Smithers.[2] I shall present here a critical reading of the tale to show, without neglecting its thematic relationship with other medieval literature (most notably *branche* IV of the Old French *Roman de Renart*), that its merits lie mainly in its delicate sense of irony.

My interpretation depends on the assumption that *FW* is really a composite of several genres. Early scholars, such as McKnight (1908, 1913) and Ker (1969:92ff) have referred to the poem in fairly neutral terms as a beast-epic, emphasizing its relationship with the Renart-cycle. Von Kreisler and Bercovitch stress the satirical elements of *FW*. Bergner, like Smithers, emphasizes the close correspondence of the text to the genre of the beast-epic, after discussing the relationship between the tale and some well-defined genres such as the fable, the fabliau and the mock-heroic or mock-romantic par-

---

[1] See especially his ample footnotes for a complete bibliography.

[2] In Bennett and Smithers (1968:65-7), preceding their edition of the text, from which all quotations from *FW* have been taken. (The translations following quotations are my own.) For a more extensive discussion of the tale in this light, see McKnight, 1913:xliii-lxi, and also McKnight, 1908:497-509.

ody. Although Bergner acknowledges the presence of fabulistic and (mock-)epic elements (1973:276-9), he clearly states that *FW* can hardly be styled epic.

In my opinion *FW* is a satire which incorporates the genre of the beast-epic, as it does those of fable, epic, and, to a lesser extent, several other prominent medieval genres such as the fabliau and even religious allegory. These several aspects ironically illuminate one another, thereby enhancing the total meaning of the poem, making it something more ambitious than a mere light-hearted animal tale. As the interplay is primarily between the widely divergent themes of epic and fable, I shall introduce my reading of *FW* with a brief discussion of these genres as they feature in it. Allusions to other genres will be mentioned as they emerge in my analysis of the text.

When *FW* is called a beast-epic it is drawn into the traditional nomenclature of the Renart-cycle, so that the term 'epic' mainly serves to link the tale to the *Roman de Renart*[3] (henceforth *RR*), which has perhaps been best described as "a loose-knit series of tales by various hands" (Cohen, 1963:34). In the comparison with *FW* we are concerned only with its *branche* IV, a 478-line episode which is introduced by its author as a *"branche"*, and furthermore as a single jest or little joke (*un sol gabet*, l.19). He contrasts it with a sermon and a saint's life (ll.4-5), and continues *C'est de Renart, bien le savez, / Et bien oï dire l'avez* (ll.21-2). It is clear that the poet of this *branche* considers it to be merely an addition to an existing, supposedly well-known narrative: 'This is about Renard, you know him well, and have surely heard talk about him'. It is only in the opening lines of *branche* II (the oldest *branche* of the cycle) that there is any discussion of the work in terms of classical epic and its medieval equivalent; this episode is compared to that between *deus barons* (l.14). Moreover, a comparison is drawn between *RR* II and the *Iliad* (l.3). We can see that there is a contrast between the authorial presentation of *branches* II and IV of *RR*.

A similar contrast is found within the small compass of *FW*. In the opening line we read: *A vox gon out of þe wode go* ('a fox came out of the wood'), and later on, when the fox is already in the well and starts howling, *Þer com a wolf gon* ... (l.108: 'there came a wolf'). The protagonists, then, are introduced in the same fashion as the animals in a fable, where the main characteristic of the animals is

---

[3] Quotations from the Roman de Renart are from Martin (1882-87).

that they are types, not individuals as in the beast-epic. No doubt the first line of *FW*, the line that would catch the attention of the medieval (as of the modern) audience or reader, would suggest a fable rather than any other genre. It is only later in the tale that identification of the protagonists takes place, resulting in the individualization of character, and also (at least to those members of the medieval audience who were familiar with the French—or Flemish—*Renart*), providing a link with the Renart-cycle. Thus, the cock is almost immediately identified as *Sire Chauntecler* (l.37). In l.128 the fox guesses *Ich wene hit is Sigrim þat Ich here* ('I think I can hear Sigrim'), and he discloses himself as *Reneuard, þi frend* (l.133: 'Renard, your friend').

The author of *FW* has, then, implicitly 'mixed' his genres of fable and beast-epic, just as in *RR* we find a similar discrepancy between *chanson de geste* and *gabet*; but whereas in the latter text this mixture of genre occurs in different *branches*, which may well have been composed by different authors, in *FW* there is only one coherent tale, in which the protagonists are first presented as fable types, and subsequently as individualized characters. The contrast between the presentation of *FW* and its corresponding *branche* of *RR* has been noticed by Bergner (1973: 270), but its importance, it seems, has been overlooked.

The English poet's mode of presenting his characters has several effects. For one thing, it shows that, although the author was basing his story on the Renart-cycle, he did not assume any great familiarity with this cycle, a fact that tallies with the few remains of Renart-poetry in medieval England. In spite of the numerous occurrences of more or less anthropomorphous foxes in medieval English art, the English of the period do not seem to have been very familiar with Renart in his literary shape.[4]

---

[4] Cf. Varty, 1967. In this book Varty adduces the evidence of 292 different artefacts based on the fox-theme as proof of his theory that "Reynard was much better known in England than extant literary evidence suggests" (p.24). Cf. also Wilson, 1952:136, which is referred to by Varty in a footnote to the above quotation. Bergner (1973: section IV, esp. 283) opposes these theories. A counter-argument that might be used here is that the MSS of very popular works may have been literally 'read to pieces'. At any rate, Bergner's statements about the absence of any assumption of popularity of the subject-matter in *FW*, especially in Chaucer's *Nun's Priest's Tale* and Caxton's translation of the Flemish *Reinaerde* seem to be convincing enough.

More important for our analysis of the tale in the light of its use of irony, however, is the impact which the gradual change-over from the fabulous to the epic mode must have made on the audience or the reader. This type of 'abuse' of genre is to be regarded as a satirical device rather than as a sign of decadence or a mishandling or misunderstanding, on the part of the author, of this theme (see, for example, Heiserman, 1961). The poet, seemingly presenting the unsuspecting reader with a fable, suddenly transforms his types into characters, characters which, as will be shown, assume an epic stature. For, after the identification of Chauntecler in 1.37, the author prepares us for the disclosing of the name of the protagonist or hero of the tale, Reneuard, by mere implication. The delayed disclosure thereby obtains the effect of an epic 'identification scene', as when Ulysses finally discloses his identity, of which the reader has been aware all along, to the Phaeacians, thereby introducing an epic element of dramatic irony.

The importance of the word *afingret* ('hungry') in 1.2, repeated in 1.4, has been stressed by Bergner (1973:270 and foot-note): it indicates the theme, which is hunger, but a hunger associated with *wo*. Perhaps Bergner has over-emphasized, in connection with these opening lines, the element of greed as *Leitmotiv*. Surely, at this stage at least the fox's hunger is natural animal appetite rather than unnatural greed such as that of the wolf. Anyway, the fox, like the wolf later on, is prepared to leave his natural habitat, the wood, and to venture into the world of man, represented by the friary. The author wittily expands the fox's concern about avoiding contact with men into an even greater concern about avoiding women, which is entirely irrelevant within the context. The joke, of course, is against women in the true medieval anti-feminist tradition, but the compari-son between hens and women suggests, ironically, that to the fox meeting a single hen is the next worse thing to meeting fifty women; it might well be, but in a different sense: Reneuard would prefer to meet half a hundred hens, or at least the five that make up Chaunte-cler's little harem.

From what follows in the poem it is clear that although the author pretends ironically that the fox is going where his nose leads him, Reneuard really knows where he is going: he recognizes the cloister wall, looks around carefully, approaches the wall and leaps in through the first breach he encounters. Although the wall has fallen down in places: *som perof wes afalle / And wes þe wal oueral tobroke* (ll.18-19: 'part of it had fallen down, and everywhere the wall was broken'), the gate of this neglected friary is locked (1.20). The order in which we are informed of the state of the cloister walls makes this passage ironic. A statement to the effect that the gate was locked, but that there were holes in the wall, would have spoiled the irony which is now upheld by the fact that the two statements are juxtaposed without any further comment. In any case, the situation is quite different in *RR* IV, where the fox has to run around and around the strong and high wall, until he finally manages to squeeze himself through a gap in the front porch (*RR* IV, ll.69-106).

The fox's laugh (1.23) seems to be one of scorn for the negligent hedge-keeper and bailiff at least as much as in exultation at the easy success of his raid so far: the human garden, supposed to be securely walled and protected, seems to have run wild.

Ironical, once again, therefore, is the fact that it is not a human being, but the cock who is the guardian of the hen-roost. The whole episode (ll.27-64) that contains the dialogue between the fox and the cock has been decried, and even called "out of proportion", especially as it seems to show some "inartistic cutting" (Wilson, 1968:248). However, it contains essential material providing links and parallels with later events in the story. A 'cutting' must of course be assumed if one reads *FW* in close connection with *RR* IV, where the fox's killing of three hens is related. But in *FW* the episode in which the fox carries the third hen along to the well, and in some versions of the story even uses it as a bait for the conviction of the wolf, does not occur. What is supposed to take place between lines 30 and 31 (Reneuard's killing and eating two of the hens) can indeed be read 'between the lines' in the ensuing debate, in which the fox answers Chauntecler's worried question: *Wat dest pou pare?* by informing him that he has only been practising a surgical operation. The effect of the absence of a factual statement about Reneuard's seizing, killing and eating of the hens is that the emphasis on the verbal battle between fox and cock is all the more prominent. In fact, the importance of dialogue, in *FW* in general, and in this part of it in particular, has been stressed by Bergner, who also emphasizes the reduction of realistic detail in comparison with *RR* IV, in favour of the 'inner realism' of the dialogue (1973:271, 273). Here, comparison with *The Nun's Priest's Tale* comes to mind, where rhetoric represents the art of persuasion *in optima forma*, and the episode with Chauntecler is therefore relevant, since it shows Reneuard's failure in this art, just as the Sigrim episode shows his success.

Besides, the Chauntecler scene shows Reneuard in his role as physician, again a traditional role, possibly the oldest of the beast-epic cycle.[5] The last line of his speech to the cock, *Oper sone axe after þe prest* (l.52: 'or else you must at once fetch a priest') ironically points forward to the role that Reneuard will presently play, and with more success. The cock, however, is not taken in.[6] Yet, in his speech his powerlessness to punish the fox physically is emphasized (*were I adoun, Ich miȝte, weste hit, he wolde* in ll.57-61 are all subjunctives). Once again, the impotence of the human element in this beast tale, the inability of man to interfere, is alluded to as well. The angrily alliterative line 62, *mid pikes and stones and staues stronge* ('with pikes and stones and heavy sticks'), is not only an idle, and therefore ironical, threat, it also ironically foreshadows line 284: *mid pikes and staues and ston—*, where the threat has now been turned into reality; only in the end it is the wolf who receives the punishment, whereas the cock has suggested it as fit for the fox (see also Von Kreisler, 1970:656-7).

Apparently, Reneuard does not expect the cock's straightforward reaction to his ironical speech; in any case, it strikes the fox completely dumb (l.65), and he will have to look elsewhere for his comfort. To account for his thirst a killing of some hens during his visit to the roost seems to be plausible, but again the author does not care to go into detail here. The fox, who does not seem to be aware of the existence of the well near-by (*Oueral he ede and sohvte*, l.69: 'he went and sought everywhere'), is yet said to be brought there by *his wiit* ('his intelligence'). This phrase, following *on auenture* ('accidentally') in the same line (l.70), must therefore be ironical. After this failure to deceive Chauntecler we are beginning to wonder how wise, or how stupid, this fox really is. This is stressed by the fox's being repeatedly reported to be non-plussed by the *ginne* of the buckets, a word that is used five times in this episode (ll.72, 77, 86, 103 and 125). The fox's lack of understanding is ironically underlined by the simple explanation on the part of the author:

> Þat wes imaked mid grete ginne.
> Tuo boketes þer he founde:

---

[5] Cf. *Ecbasis Captivi* (ca. 940), Nivardus' *Isengrimus* (ca. 1149), and *RR* IV.
[6] Another traditional feature; cf. the Sprotinus episode in *Isengrimus*, and *The Nun's Priest's Tale*. The fox outwitted by the cock is another fable-motif: cf. Marie de France, *Fables*, No. 60: *Del cok e del gupil*.

Þat oþer wende to þe grounde,
Þat wen me shulde þat on opwinde
Þat oþer wolde adoun winde.   (72-6)

(Which was built with great ingenuity. Two buckets he found there:
one of them went to the bottom, in such a way that when one
wound up one, the other would go down.)

... *grete ginne* indeed!

The author now proceeds to taunt his hero with his lack of
understanding of simple mechanics. Lines 77-95 are a slow but
steady exposure of an almost predestined downfall (*Adoun he moste,
he wes perinne*—, 1.85: 'he had to go down, as he was ''in for it''');
the fox has, as it were, pressed the fatal button, he has put into
motion (a downward motion) the *swikele ginne* that will later on
become the instrument of his own treachery towards the wolf. Perhaps also the *swikele ginne* ('treacherous device') serves as a parody
of the epic machinery; the literal 'machinery' certainly has a myste-
rious superiority, a super-animal (because human) quality, with
which neither fox nor wolf should really meddle.

In a speech full of proverbial cliché (ll.96-106) the fox now
indulges in self-pity rather than self-accusation. Again one senses the
parody, this time of the epic hero's self-condemnatory speech when
he feels he has let his fellows down. Yet, like a true Ulysses or
Aeneas, Reneuard steels himself against his misfortune when the
wolf is brought on stage. Like the fox, he has ventured *Out of þe
depe wode* (1.109).[7] The meeting of heroes will now soon take place,
and after this the great battle, which is one of words (Bergner, 1973:
278). But first there is the identification scene. The wolf, who is said
to have immediately recognized the fox by his voice (ll.114-16), still
asks, *pro forma* as it were, who it is down there, and adds irony by
asking: *Hertou Cristine oþer mi fere?* (1.120: 'Are you a Christian or
my friend?'). The second irony (the first is that of the feigned non-
recognition) is, however, directed at the wolf himself: anyone who is
his friend cannot be a Christian. A third level of irony can be
adduced if the line is regarded as foreshadowing the fox's impersson-
ating of the Christian *par excellence*, the priest.[8] The wolf's exhorta-

---

[7] Incidentally, the phrase *out of þe (...) wode* is the only reminiscence in *FW* of the
Isengrimus: *egrediens silua mane Ysengrimus* (l.1).

[8] Perhaps it should also be borne in mind that traditionally the *wolf* is often referred
to (in *Isengrimus* and in *RR*) as a monk or even an abbot.

tion to the fox to *gabbe* [him] *nout* ('do not deceive him'), which is exactly what Reneuard is going to do, is another example of dramatic irony.

   With the fox's recognition of his *kun* his *wiit* returns (ll.123-4). The word *ginne* is used for the trick that is going to bring the wolf down and the fox up. But the latter needs time, and therefore the recognition scene is prolonged. 'Aren't you Sigrim?' 'Yes indeed, but who are you?' 'I'll tell you, no lies: I am Reneuard, your friend' (ll.127-33). The very first apposition to Reneuard's proper name is a lie: Reneuard is neither Sigrim's 'kinsman' nor his 'friend', as will soon appear. By introducing the word *ibede* in l.135 the fox is gradually entering upon his role as a (mock-)priest. Ironically, his self-accusation in ll.96-106 had already placed him in the light of one who is about to enter upon a holy life (see Bercovitch, 1966:290-91), and the parody of religious instruction, which the fox significantly starts in l.139 with the remark *Þou art ounwiis!* ('you are stupid!') culminates in a fine example of the unctuous hypocrisy of friardom in ll.158-66.

   The doubtful wolf, wondering what *he* should do in the well, is told by the fox that *Her is þe blisse of Paradiis* (l.140: 'here is the bliss of Paradise'). At this stage the fox is not yet suggesting that he actually *is* in paradise, but that the well is *like* paradise—he is obviously 'thinking aloud'. His first, vague description of the food and drink to be found in good abundance at the bottom of what seems to be an ordinary well merely makes the wolf laugh (l.148). He, too, takes the fox's words as ironical: 'Come off it—if that's true you must be dead—'. No reply. Beginning to wonder whether the fox can really be dead, it is now the wolf who is thinking aloud: 'I saw you and your family not three days ago!' But was not three days the time it took for Christ to die, to descend into Hell and rise again? The collective dinner at the wolf's becomes suddenly reminiscent of the Last Supper, and the fox prepares himself and us for his Resurrection by associating himself with Christ in l.159. The dense wolf, of course, is unaware of the fact that in this little allegory the well stands for Hell, not Paradise, nor does he recognize in the fox's further specification of the *mete* of l.143 into *shep and get* (l.167) an allusion to the last Judgment. By now, further religious and allegorical allusions, such as that to the well of Jacob (see Bercovitch, 1966:290), and also the immediate link a medieval audience would establish between a pit and the entrance to hell, have given an extra ironical framework to the dialogue. But the development of the plot

turns vitally at l.170. The sheep and goats remind the wolf, not of
these Christian allusions to virtue and vice, good and evil, but of his
own insatiable hunger. He is now morally blinded and ready to follow any instructions the fox may give. When the wolf mentions for-
giving the fox's crimes against him, the latter immediately takes him
up on this idea, reversing the procedure: the wolf shall 'confess' to
the fox and be absolved by him. Reneuard can even afford to refuse
shrift to the wolf at first, Sigrim is so willing: *Ich wot, toniȝt Ich
worpe ded, / Bote pou do me somne reed* (ll.191-2: 'I am sure I shall
die this night unless you give me some advice'). Again, this is dramatic irony, because the fox's counsel will almost be the death of the
wolf.

The confession scene (ll.199-228) is one of the most complex
passages in the whole poem. The wolf now reveals himself in his full
stupidity and appears much as the self-confessing Vice of later
drama, as a braggart, and as a pretended hero, the first by his phrase
Ich habbe ben qued al mi lif-daie (l.200: 'I have been wicked all my
life'), the last by the next line *ich habbe widewene kors*— ('I have
the curse of widows'): the widows' curse, apart from its biblical
overtone, is reminiscent of the epic formula in which a battle is
reported to be the cause of grief of the widows of the slain. Sigrim
has killed a thousand sheep, he boasts (l.203), and the widows, one
presumes, are the ewes. In reality, perhaps, the widows are the
unfortunate owners of the sheep stolen by the wolf, the likes of the
povre wydwe in Chaucer's *Nun's Priest's Tale*.

In all likelihood, however, the wolf has not *abiten* his *pousent
shep* at one go, as an epic hero would kill his anonymous rabble-
victims, but in the course of his life, and the figure is, of course,
epic hyperbole anyway. One wonders whether the weight of the
satirical attack is not here rather against the contemporary epic-
romance than against the braggart-wolf. One remembers in this
context the hyperbolic numbers said to be slain by Roland at his last
stand: at first 20,000 against 400,000, the French are later sixty
against 50,000, and Roland is repeatedly reported to attack his adversaries by the score.[9] Significantly, it is not the author as com-
mentator, but Sigrim himself who exaggerates the number of his
victims.

---

[9] Cf. also Brooke, 1969:158: "In the popular theology of the late eleventh and early
twelfth centuries, ... the heathen were cattle for the slaughter."

From Sigrim the braggart-hero we proceed to Sigrim the cuckold. Lines 211-20 seem to contain an allusion to Reneuard the courtly lover (cf. *RR* IV, 1.160, where Renart thinks he sees in the well Hermeline, *Sa famme qu'aime d'amor fine* ('his wife, whom he loves chivalrously'), a paradoxical statement in the light of the 'rules' of courtly love). The episode, of course, is a remnant of the reflection-in-the-water theme in *RR* IV. In the wolf's speech, the supreme irony is his remark that he thought, like everybody else, *that þat Ich iseie were soþ* (1.218: 'what I saw should be true'), while he is actually looking down on Reneuard attempting to deceive him from the bottom of a well which he passes off as Paradise. What else remains to the fox but to forgive his dupe at *pisse nede* (1.225: 'in this need')? The wolf's reaction is typical: now that he is *in clene liue* (1.227: 'in a way of life free from sin') he no longer cares a straw for wife or children: a truly un-Christian point of view.

The fox now informs the wolf that the top-bucket is a *bruche of heuene blisse* (1.233: 'an opening into the bliss of heaven'), and so it is indeed, but for the fox, not the wolf. The latter, with characteristic denseness, says: *Þat is liȝt to done!* (1.236: 'that is easy to do!'), when it is really his weight that is his literal downfall. Of course, the fox has realized that the wolf is heavier than he, and so he ascends while the wolf, half suspecting that there is something wrong here, comes down. Reneuard's farewell speech is nastily ironic. Still in his pretended role as a priest he promises to ring the wolf's death-knell (the clattering of the wolf's bucket on to the bottom?). A litotes and a nasty metaphor conclude this passage, and so we take our leave of the fox with the remark that he cared little about what happened to the wolf (1.260), an ironic remark seeing that the fox had previously taken upon himself the two roles of the physician, who is supposed to take care of the body, and the priest, who does the same for the soul.

Sigrim, however, is not yet through with his ordeal. The description of his state, *afringet so þat he ves wod* (1.285: 'so hungry that he was mad (madly ravenous)'), has almost become formulaic. *Inou he cursede þat þider him broute* (1.259: 'he often cursed the one who had brought him to that position'): if he is quite fair, it is himself he is cursing, not Reneuard.

Then, at last, the human world intervenes. It has seemed superfluous to discuss what has gone before in terms of anti-clerical satire, since this has been done by Bercovitch (1966) and Von Kreisler (1970). But the third part of the triptych which forms *FW*, the punishment of Sigrim (ll.261-95), has not been regarded in this light by previous students of this poem, though there is every reason for doing so. In this episode, Sigrim 'merely' receives his traditional corporal punishment (in *Isengrimus* he ultimately dies of his wounds), but the *sley* friars do not get away unscathed either. The neglect of their grounds has already been mentioned. Ironically, it is Ailmer the gardener, who would have been responsible for the upkeep of the garden walls (and therefore not 'less appropriately', as Smithers states in a note to 1.59 [Bennett and Smithers, 1968:300]), who, shirking his duty of singing matins, discovers Sigrim when he goes to the well to quench his thirst. He mistakes Sigrim for the devil, and this links the episode to the confession scene earlier on: much as Sigrim had taken the well to be the entrance to heavenly paradise, so the friars superstitiously mistake it for the exit of hell. Their 'reaction' to the appearance of the 'devil' is physical, rather than spiritual. The poem ends on a harsh note, with the friars beating and stabbing the wolf—without *forʒeuenesse* (1.295), of which they are possibly incapable.[10] In their duping of Sigrim the 'real' friars are not much better than the false priest Reneuard.

As I have suggested earlier on, it is the combination of fable material and epic treatment that makes the beast-epic into a potential satire. In *FW*, the reader is presented with two traditional fables (the fox and the cock in the tree, the fox and the wolf in the well), upon which is superimposed the characterisation of the protagonists: the types of a cock, a fox and a wolf assume identities, and become the characters Chauntecler, Reneuard and Sigrim. In the 'ordinary' epic, the hero is a superhuman, usually national, character, who serves as an example, to which, however, we can never really hope to live up, although we are meant to. In the beast-epic, which is really a variety of the mock-epic, the hero is either a mock-hero or an anti-hero. Both variants are represented in *FW*. Reneuard, who is the 'hero' of the French cycle called after him, is an anti-hero. He is admirable, but in an adverse way. He does not, I think, bear the brunt of the author's anti-clerical satire, as Bercovitch seems to suggest (1966: 288), although part of the time he certainly stands for the corrupt cleric. But one of the relevancies of the Chauntecler episode is that it shows us Reneuard in another role, that of the physician, in the Middle Ages, as now, a ready object of satire. More importantly, *FW* shows us, in Reneuard's relation to the other two characters, that the

---

[10] Cf. the emphasis on forgiveness in the confession scene (ll.175, 225).

success of the evil anti-hero is not entirely in his own hands, but is largely dependent on the quality of his antagonists.

Sigrim, the 'larger' of Reneuard's opponents, is far more than "the duped layman" (Bercovitch, 1966:288). He is even more than the "stupid, greedy, ever-hungry Wolf without whom the equally greedy but far more cunning Fox could not survive" (Von Kreisler, 1970:658). He is a mock-hero, a would-be epic hero like his predecessor Isengrimus in Nivardus' poem, or a would-be medieval nobleman as in the *Ecbasis Captivi*. Miserable failure is his eternal reward. Where Reneuard succeeds on his wanderings that even lead him down to a mock-epic Underworld, the well, Sigrim fails. That the quest is always one for food or drink rather than for a city to be founded or destroyed, or for a Holy Grail, only emphasizes the mockery inherent in the beast-epic.

Obviously, it is hard for us to identify with either of these 'heroes' (Bergner, (1973:276). Perhaps, therefore, the real hero of the tale is Chauntecler, whose claim has thus far been neglected. The disadvantage of this suggestion is that the cock is not really very heroic. He fails to protect his hens against the onslaught of the fox. He refuses to come down like a true hero and fight Reneuard, even against the odds. But then all fighting in *FW*, except the beating up of Sigrim by the friars, is verbal rather than physical. And in his verbal battle with Reneuard Chauntecler has the upper hand.

Perhaps we must see in *FW* an attempt on the part of a learned poet to decry the epic heroes in favour of the commonsensical point of view. Needless to say, this aspect of *FW* is subservient to the moral one that is inherent in the fable material in the tale. But by combining the two fables, adding the protagonists' identities, and placing the whole within a human framework, the author of *FW* has, like Chaucer in his *Nun's Priest's Tale*, done more than compose "merely a humorous beast-fable" (Tucker, 1908:109). He has presented his audience with an ironical satire in which to the simple plots of the two fables (traditionally dealing with the consequences of verbal trickery), are added the pretences of characters addicted to rhetoric: boasting heroes, hypocritical clerics and intellectual but ineffectual quacks. Thus, epic action is reduced to mock-epic action on the one hand (the entirely senseless descent of the two 'heroes' into the well), and to idle and immoral verbosity on the other (the dialogues). As has been shown, the poetic medium used to obtain the effect of verbal deceit that pervades *FW*, is bound up with its irony.

Seemingly a mock-serious, even light-hearted animal tale, the poem is really a serious satire on human deceitfulness.

REFERENCES

Bennett, J.A.W., and G.V. Smithers (eds.) (1968). *Early Middle English Verse and Prose*. 2nd ed. Oxford: O.U.P. (1st ed., 1966).

✴Bercovitch, S. (1966). Clerical Satire in þe Vox and þe Wolf. *JEGP* 65. 287-94.

Bergner, H. (1973). *The Fox and the Wolf* und die Gattung des Tierepos in der mittelenglischen Literatur. *Germanisch-Romanische Monatschrift* 23. 268-85.

Brooke, C. (1969). *The Twelfth Century Renaissance*. London: Thames and Hudson.

Cohen, J.M. (1963). *A History of Western Literature*. Rev. ed. Chicago: Albine.

Heiserman, A.R. (1961). *Skelton and Satire*. Chicago: University of Chicago Press.

Ker, W.P. (1969). *Medieval English Literature*. Oxford: O.U.P. (1st publ. 1912).

Martin, E. (ed.) (1882-87). *Roman de Renart*. 3 Vols. Strasbourg.

McKnight, G.H. (1908). The Middle English Vox and Wolf. *PMLA* 23. 497-509.

McKnight, G.H. (ed.) (1913). *Middle English Humorous Tales in Verse*. Boston and London: D.C. Heath.

Tucker, S.M. (1908). *Verse Satire in England before the Renaissance*. Columbia University Studies in English. New York.

Varty, K. (1967). *Reynard the Fox: A Study of the Fox in Medieval Art*. Leicester: Leicester U.P.

✴Von Kreisler, N. (1970). Satire in *The Fox and the Wolf*. *JEGP* 69. 650-58.

Wilson, R.M. (1952). *The Lost Literature of Medieval England*. London: Methuen.

Wilson, R.M. (1968). *Early Middle English Literature*. 3rd ed. London: Methuen.

THE LAND OF COKAYGNE
SOPHISTICATED MIRTH

WIM TIGGES
(University of Leiden)

As is often the case with texts whose impact is mainly of a comical or mildly satirical nature, the Middle English "lay" of *The Land of Cokaygne* (henceforth *LC*) has been either neglected altogether or only mentioned in passing. It has received little critical attention. Early editors and critics concentrate on its Irish provenance, and on its relationship with the Old French *Fabliau de Cocagne* and the Middle Dutch *Dit is van dat edele Land van Cockaengen*.[1] The poem has been most convincingly referred to as a satire, a parody and a burlesque (see respectively Zesmer, 1961:186, Bennett and Smithers, 1968:137, and Blake, 1977:127), but it has also been noted to contain elements of a (goliardic) Utopia (see Pearsall, 1977:100, and especially Morton, 1978:15-25). This variety of interpretations seems to indicate a certain complexity of meaning. To the folk motif of the Delectable Land the poet has added a satirical element, which has led Kuczynski (1980:45-55) to the conclusion that the poem is both a Utopia and a satire. In the same article he also comments on the mixture of Celtic and Germanic material concerning a place which is untroubled by the vicissitudes of earthly life (1980:50-51), and comes to the conclusion that the poem was intended for a mixed audience. In this paper I intend to demonstrate that by collating a wide variety of traditions of the Delectable land and by adopting a sophisticated diction characteristic of courtly romance, the poet presents what is essentially a folk-tale, but informed with an ironic view of an essential element in human life: the desire for an escape to a never-never-land, no matter whether of supreme materialism

---

[1] The OF analogue, and part of the MDu one, have been edited and discussed by Väänänen (1947). The two known versions of the MDu poem can be found in Priebsch (1894). The so-called Kildare poems, to which *LC* belongs, were first edited and discussed by Heuser (1904). For the history and affiliations of the folktale elements, see Poeschel (1878) and Bolte and Polivka (1918:iii.244ff).

(abundant food, clothes and sex), asceticism (the monastery) or chivalry (the romantic pleasance).

One aspect of the poem's sophistication is the superimposition of at least nine variants of the Other World.[2] The traditions with which the poet seems to demonstrate familiarity are: **1** The folk tradition of the land of "Fair Ease", whose bliss consists in a superfluity of food and drink, separated from the outside world by an unpleasant, almost insurmountable obstacle. It is this tradition which links *LC* to the OF and MDu analogues. **2** The Earthly Paradise of Christian legend, with which Cokaygne is favourably compared. **3** The Celtic myth of the Blessed Isles, like those visited by St Brendan. **4** Related to this, the fabulous western islands described in the Old Irish travelogues or *Immrama*, describing the voyages of legendary travellers such as Bran, Mael Dúin and the Uí Chorra. **5** The parodies of these travelogues, as presented in *The Vision of Mac-Conglinne*. It is the apparent acquaintance of the poet with the last three traditions that supports the theory that the poem is of Irish derivation, as argued in particular by Henry (1972:120-41). **6** The classical account of the Golden Age, as found in the first book of Ovid's *Metamorphoses* and in Virgil's *Fourth Eclogue*. **7** The medieval tradition of the *locus amoenus*, the enclosed pleasance of romance tradition. **8** The notion of the cloister as a paradise, which is discussed by Henry and especially by Hill (1975:55-6). It is this element in particular which creates a certain ambiguity in the possible interpretation of the poem, since the cloister could be regarded in this way from a favourable point of view: as an ideal, self-sufficient community, but also from the unfavourable point of view of the disappointed layman or the disillusioned cleric: as a self-centred and pleasure-loving society. **9** A possible reference to the Islamic paradise with its accommodating *houris* (see Metlitzki, 1977:210-19).[3]

It may well be the case, as Henry suggests (1972:134ff), that the author of *LC* was a Franciscan criticizing the all-too-worldly

---

[2] For my discussion of this topic I am greatly indebted to Patch (1950). See also Baring-Gould, 1977:89-91.

[3] In the light of the theory, never satisfactorily proved but not definitively rejected either, that most medieval humorous tales, especially those like the *fabliaux*, where the humour is connected with an erotic theme or plot, are ultimately derived from the East, the potential presence of an undercurrent of Eastern material should, I think, be taken into account. (Cf. Benfey, 1859.)

behaviour of Cistercian monks in a particular Irish cloister. However, the total effect of the poem transcends such a limited reading.
Therefore I shall endeavour to demonstrate how the poet satirizes
the human desire for escape in general by means of a sophisticated,
courtly diction, and, by doing that, burlesques in passing the types of
text, popular with a fairly general audience, that accommodate this
desire by a frequently facile indulgence in wish-fulfilment: the romance, the fabliau, the travelogue, and even the account of a delectable place after death.

The author of *LC* sets out to describe a land better than St
Brendan's Island, better even than the Earthly Paradise: *Þoȝ Paradis
be miri and briȝt,/ Cokaygn is of fairir siȝt* (ll.5-6: 'Although Paradise be delightful and beautiful, Cokaygne is more beautiful to look
upon').[4] Instead of enumerating the assets of Cokaygne, he now proceeds to decry those of Eden (ll.7-16), but there does not seem to be
so much difference after all: as in Paradise, also in Cokaygne there
are neither care nor labour (l.18), no nightfall (l.26), no discord
(l.27), no death (l.28), and no harmful animals (l.31). But at this
stage the poet begins to overdo things. From the absence of serpent,
wolf and fox, he proceeds to less obnoxious animals one would not
mind encountering in a land of bliss, unless one happens to be a
refined aristocrat, monk or otherwise, secluded in the ivory tower of
castle or cloister: horse, cow, sheep, swine, goat. Clearly the land of
Cokaygne is no pastoral world, nor is it a world in which animals
provide toil and trouble.

By the time we reach ll.37-8: *Nis per flei, fle, no lowse / In
clop, in toune, bed, no howse* ('There is neither fly, flea nor louse in
clothing, city, bed or house'), one begins to have doubts as to the
poet's noblemindedness; after a series of traditional, rhetorical nega-
tions (see, for example, Patch, 1950:171, and Hill, 1975:57) a stage
of bathos has suddenly been reached. By his continuation, however,
the poet suggests that he is doing no more than simply denying the
presence of any unpleasant elements: nasty weather and blindness are
as absent as the muck which is the consequence of keeping cattle.
This subtle shifting of tone is a first indication of the mixture of
genres the poet is employing all through the poem. At one level he is
repeating the topic of the "seven joys of heaven" with its obverse

---

[4] All quotations from *LC* have been taken from Bennett and Smithers, 1968:136-
44.

catalogue, at another he is parodying this very idea by giving it a slightly absurd bias, and at a third he is pointing forward to the folk-loristic catalogue of ll.51-64, itself possibly a parody of the romantic one of ll.65-100.

In the first 50 lines we find nothing that is really absurd. Of course, the description of Cokaygne is entirely unrealistic, but then the land is a kind of Earthly Paradise, only superior. The connection is made by the mention of Paradise in l.5, by the allusions already mentioned, and also by the reference to the four conventional characteristics of Earthly Paradise, the four rivers, the soft climate, the fruitful soil and its being the dwelling place of Enoch and Elias.

But, while the *riuers gret and fine/ Of oile, melk, honi, and wine* (ll.44-5) can be easily accepted as metaphors of natural or rather supernatural opulence, abbey walls made of pasties (l.54) defy such a reading. With the opening of the second section (ll.51-100) the author has definitely turned to folkloristic Cokaygne imagery, that of buildings made of food, and we may now see retrospectively that the rivers were meant to anticipate this, and that their contents have to be taken literally. What is particularly interesting is that the food imagery is much less prominent than in the OF analogue, and further that it is associated with a monastery.[5] It is at this stage, too, that the satire begins, since the poem clearly suggests that the white and grey monks, of whatever order they be, are living in a kind of cloud-cuckoo-land.

To a layman, this must have been a recognizable picture of any monastery, to judge by the multifarious examples of anti-monastic criticism of the later Middle Ages. The monastery was a kind of island in society, secluded from the surrounding world by its walls, "ideally a replica of heaven on earth" (Southern, 1970:230), and in any case a veritable *paradisus claustralis* (Hill, 1975:56). Particularly interesting, in the light of the mention made of the four rivers in l.45 of *LC*, the spices (ll.73-8) and the roses and lilies (ll.79-80), is the description by Peter Damien in addressing Abbot Hugh of Cluny: "I saw a *Paradise* ... watered by the *four streams* of the Gospels, overflowing with spiritual virtues. I saw a garden bringing forth all kinds of delicious *roses and lilies*, heavy with the sweet fragrance of scents and *spices*, ... (Southern, 1970:230, italics mine).

---

[5] For a discussion of the identity of the white and grey monks of l.52, see note to l.164 in Bennett and Smithers, 1968:341. For an interesting discussion of "white canons" (the Premonstratensians) and their double monasteries, see Heer, 1974:60.

We can also see a link between the cloister as the "gate of Paradise" (Heer, 1974:56) or even Paradise itself, and the excessive consumption of food by monks. On the latter aspect Heer informs us that "From very primitive times honouring the dead has taken the form of ceremonious eating and drinking" (1974:52) and so we are led to assume that "The complaints about the intemperate eating and drinking among monks and collegiate clergy, which in the twelfth century became increasingly strident (...) must be seen in this context" (1974:52-3). Of course, what comes to mind here is the Irish tradition of the "Wake".

In *LC*, the monastery is a mixture of the "traditional" Co-kaygne (ll.54-66) and of the *locus amoenus* of medieval romance, which abounds in precious stones (ll.67-70, 88-94), exotic spices (ll.71-8), the traditional roses and lilies (ll.79-82), the medicinal fountain (ll.83-7) and bird-song (ll.95-100). The whole section, which is purely descriptive, reads like a parody of similar episodes in romances, an exaggeration of the rhetorical device of the cata-logue. From the "vulgar" catalogue of puddings and pies the poet shifts almost imperceptibly to the aristocratic one of gems and ginger: even the food-list is not quite so common as the title of the poem would suggest. Far from describing the everyday fare of the common man, or the frugal diet of the monastery, the poet enumer-ates the items on an aristocratic *menu*, a fact which, together with the sophisticated vocabulary in which this section is couched, points to a type of audience which was all too familiar with the courtly way of life.[6]

Just when this audience imagines it has left the land of Ready-made and finds itself on familiar ground in the romantic pleasance, the author once again takes up the food imagery. This time the audi-ence is asked to believe that roasted geese fly into the abbey, an-nouncing themselves with what was no doubt a familiar street-cry, or rather, a subtle variation of one: *Gees, al hote, al hot!* (1.104). These geese, and their equally obliging colleagues the larks (1.107) were no doubt suggested by the previous catalogue of the pleasance birds; the numerous singing birds, several of which are mentioned in ll.96-7, are contrasted to the cooking birds of ll.102-10. Likewise

---

[6] The number of French-derived words in *LC* is surprisingly high, being around 10.5% of the total lexis. There are 24 words in *LC* which the *OED* gives as first recorded in this text. Many of these are from the fields of cooking and the lapidary.

the *gilofre* ('clove') and *canel* ('cinnamon') with which they season themselves (l.110) are ready to hand in the pleasance (cf. ll.76-7).

In the next episode (ll.113-46) the monks' style of living is recounted. It proves to be that of the courtly romantic lover. The poet emphasizes that the monks are young (l.121), and they are so *heiʒ of mode* (l.125: 'high-spirited') that they actually take off from the ground and fly. Their sleeves and hoods remind not only the abbot of real birds—no doubt the author is touching upon a familiar sight: these monks are wearing the fashionable wide-sleeved tunics. The whole passage is very reminiscent of Chaucer's description of the Squire in the General Prologue to *The Canterbury Tales* (ll.79-100; Robinson, 1957:18). The squire, too, is young (l. 79), his tunic has *sleves longe and wyde* (l.93) and he is even compared to a bird (ll.91, 98). The common source of both passages is presumably the *Roman de la Rose*, where the ideal young lover is extensively described (ll.2075-220; Lecoy, 1970).

In the description of the abbot's futile attempt to get his underlings back to earth (ll.133-46) the courtly atmosphere is somewhat debunked. The whole scene is remarkably reminiscent of savages beating and dancing around war-drums, and may be compared in its presentation to the garbled accounts in the romance of *Kyng Alisaunder* or in *Mandeville's Travels*. Henry (1972:136) connects this scene with the *pulsatio tabule* to waken monks in the morning. The flying, I think, is meant to allude to the fact that these monks not only offend against the vows of poverty, chastity and obedience (cf. Hill, 1975:55) but also against that of stability of place.

In fact, the monks' doings as described in this passage are as much subject to daily regulation as ordinary monastic life: first they say mass (they are not entirely idle in their religious observance, although they seem to skip the inconveniently early lauds and matins), next they take to their flying games, which take the place of the manual or intellectual labour required of real-life monks (cf. Hill, 1975:57-8). The exuberant dancing around the *maidin* ('girl') also seems to have the marks of a regular habit, and so off to their *collacione* ('light evening meal').

The fourth section of *LC* (ll.147-82) begins by describing the nunnery. The nuns, too, are young (l.152), and the river of sweet milk (l.149) seems the most appropriate of the four streams mentioned in ll.45-6 for the nunnery to be situated on. Initially, the sweet milk, the boating, and the naked swimming seem to emphasize their innocence (or chastity: Hill, 1975:58). But the young monks are there to "instruct" them (l.165). The account of the goings-on between the nuns and the monks takes us back once more to folkloristic Cokaygne, where not only food and drink, but also abundant sex is an important asset, as in the OF analogue. As is usual in medieval texts of the nature of a fabliau, the act of intercourse is euphemistically paraphrased, in this case in terms of prayer (*oreisun*, l.165) and dancing (*iambleue*, l.166), thereby emphasizing not only the oral and genital aspects of physical love, but also once again the clerical and courtly aspects.

To some extent the episode is in accordance with the criticism that might be incurred by the institution of the double monastery, once a characteristic feature of Irish monasticism and partially revived in England during the twelfth century (Heer, 1974:60). Once more, anti-monastic satire is presented. The absence of even the mildest anti-feminist satire may be attributed to the chivalric outlook of the poet.

Having concluded his description of Cokaygne by alluding to another folkloristic feature, also found in the OF analogue, that excessive sleep as culmination of laziness is rewarded (ll.173-7), the poet ends on a note which seems to be as (mildly) defensive of monastic life as the preceding episodes have been (mildly) satirical of it. The seven years' penance is comparable to the traditional mountain of rice pudding in the later Dutch analogue of *Luilekkerland*, first recorded in 1546. In general, it stands for the near-insurmountable obstacles that protect these delectable places against easy and frequent visitation from outside. More specifically, the passage (ll.177-82) leads us back to the world of religion which sets the tone of the poem. Translated into religious precepts, the symbols of Cokaygne and the swine's dung teach us that we must accept a life of hardship and overcome obstacles on our path before we can enter the abode of heavenly bliss. In terms of common psychology the meaning of these symbols is that in order to lead a balanced life one must take the rough with the smooth, a common enough precept, but seldom presented in such an original way.

Even in relation to monastic life the seven years' wading in swine's dung makes sense: it may stand for the period of tedious study during the novitiate, or perhaps more generally for the material hardship that monastic life entailed. In his final prayer, the author makes it clear that the unpleasant side of life can be seen as a penance. He also seems to imply that the good life he has so exuberantly described can be experienced in *this* world (ll.184-5). On the other hand, the very absurdity of the nature of the "penance" finally shows up the impossibility of ever being able to escape towards the Delectable Land—unless one inhabits it already, by belonging to the secular or clerical aristocracy.

REFERENCES

Baring-Gould, S. (1977). *Curious Myths of the Middle Ages*. London: Jupiter Books. (1st publ., 1866.)
Benfey, T. (1859). *Pantschatantra*. Leipzig.
Bennett, J.A.W. and G.V. Smithers (eds.) (1968). *Early Middle English Verse and Prose*. 2nd ed. Oxford: O.U.P. (1st ed., 1966)
Blake, N. (1977). *The English Language in Medieval Literature*. London: Methuen.
Bolte, J. and G. Polivka (1918). *Anmerkungen zu den Kinder- und Hausmärchen der Brüder Grimm*. Leipzig.
Heer, F. (1974). *The Medieval World. Europe 1100-1350*. Transl. J. Sondheimer. London: Sphere Books. (1st publ., 1962.)
✻ Henry, P.L. (1972). The Land of Cokaygne: Cultures in Contact in Medieval Ireland. *Studia Hibernica* 12. 120-41.
Heuser, W. (1904). *Die Kildare-Gedichte*. Bonn: Hanstein [Bonner Beiträge zur Anglistik 14]. 1904. (Repr. Darmstadt, 1965.)
✻ Hill, T.D. (1975). Parody and Theme in the Middle English "Land of Cokaygne". *Notes and Queries* 220. 55-59.
Kuczynski, P. (1980). Utopie und Satire in *The Land of Cokaygne. Zeitschrift für Anglistik und Amerikanistik* 28. 45-55.
Lecoy, F. (ed.) (1970). *Roman de la Rose*. Paris: Champion.
Metlitzki, D. (1977). The Muslim Paradise as the Land of Cokaygne. In: *The Matter of Araby in Medieval England*. New Haven and London: Yale U.P. 210-19.
Morton, A.L. (1978). *The English Utopia*. London: Lawrence and Wishart. (1st publ., 1952.)
Patch, H.R. (1950). *The Other World According to Descriptions in Medieval Literature*. Smith College Studies in Modern Languages. New Series. Cambridge, MA.
Pearsall, D. (1977). *Old and Middle English Poetry*. London: Routledge and Kegan Paul.
Poeschel, J. (1878). Das Märchen vom Schlaraffenlande. *Beiträge zur Geschichte der deutschen Sprache und Literatur* 5. 389-427.
Priebsch, R. (1894). Noch einmal 'Van dat edele lant van Cockaengen'. *Tijdschrift voor Nederlandse Taal- en Letterkunde* 13. 185-91.
Robinson, F.N. (ed.) (1958). *The Works of Geoffrey Chaucer*. 2nd ed. London: O.U.P. (1st ed., 1933.)
Southern, R.W. (1970). *Western Society and the Church in the Middle Ages*. Harmondsworth: Penguin Books.

Väänänen, V. (1947). Le fabliau de Cocagne. *Neuphilologische Mitteilungen* 48. 3-36.

Zesmer, D.M. (1961). *Guide to English Literature. From Beowulf through Chaucer and Medieval Drama.* New York: Barnes and Noble.

LORE, LIFE, AND LOGIC
IN
THE OWL AND THE NIGHTINGALE *

JUDITH C. PERRYMAN
(Leiden, d. 1985)

The early thirteenth-century Middle English work *The Owl and the Nightingale*, the first of a number of bird debates in English, is an outstanding and interesting poem, none the less because there has been so much controversy about its meaning.[1] Though the interpretation of it may be troublesome, its humour and lively argument give it great appeal. The birds as they reveal themselves as characters are at once infuriating and likeable, cantankerous and restrained, timid, angry and exultant. They seem like squabbling children who are to be understood and controlled rather than heard and respected, and who need a mature mind to intervene and reconcile them. That is the role of the elusive Nicholas of Guildford, possible author of the poem, who is the man with whom the final judgment will rest. He receives high praise in the poem for his wisdom (ll.1755-6) and diplomacy, for his hatred of vice, and for his lack of rashness in dealing with it (ll.192-3).[2] The only point about which almost every critic seems to be agreed is that the poem is a plea for the personal preferment of Nicholas because of his capacity as arbitrator. But what he has to arbitrate about and what is the precise theme of the poem has been the subject of many varying opinions.

There are a number of important issues raised in the poem that were of current interest: They include, as Lumiansky puts it (1953: 415):

> ... love, honest and illicit, and marriage ... new love poetry and the traditional didactic religious poetry ...

---

* Reprinted, with kind permission from the editors, from *Dutch Quarterly Review of Anglo-American Letters* 14 (1984). 97-109.
[1] For an account of the poem and full bibliography, see Utley (1972:716-20, 874-82).
[2] Citations throughout are from Stanley (1960).

> astrology and witchcraft ... new gentle preaching as
> opposed to the old thundering sermon ... ascendancy of
> wisdom over strength and ... the folly of warfare.

The drawback in looking for what Nicholas' judgment might be on
any of these topics is that the points in the argument are presented so
murkily by the birds, and the level of debate is so low.

The various views expressed by the birds in the course of discussing these questions have led to a number of other ideas both
about the subject of Nicholas' judgment and about which bird he will
favour. It has been suggested that the debate may be a contest
between gloom and joy, or a confrontation between philosophy and
art, orthodoxy and heresy, the cleric and the minstrel, or practical-
ism and idealism, to name a few.[3]

The most convincing interpretation to date to encompass in a
satisfying way not only the variety of views and topics covered in the
poem but also its tone is that developed by Kathryn Hume in the last
chapters of her book *The Owl and the Nightingale* (1975). She looks
upon the poem as a burlesque satire on human contentiousness, a
theme stated early on in the poem in the lines:

> "Ac lete we awei þos cheste,
> Vor suiche wordes boþ unwerste
> & fo we on mid riȝte dome,
> Mid faire worde & mid ysome.
> Þeȝ we ne bo at one acorde
> We muȝe bet mid fayre worde,
> Witute cheste & bute fiȝte,
> Plaidi mid foȝe & mid riȝte;
> & mai hure eiþer wat hi wile
> Mid riȝte segge & mid sckile."   (177-86)

("But let us cast off this strife, for words such as these are of no
avail, and let us begin with rightful judgment with gracious and
peaceable words. Although we are not in agreement, we shall be
able better, with gracious words and without strife or conflict, to
plead with propriety and justness. And let each of us do what she
wishes with truthful speech and with reason.")

---

[3] For a summary of various interpretations, see Kathryn Hume (1975:10-12).

This theme is consistently borne out to the poem's inconclusive end.[4]

In presenting this theme through talking creatures the poet had not only the natural qualities of these two familiar birds to call on to provide the basis of the characters but also the traditional lore explaining the habits and significance of each. Indeed, he could not ignore this lore. He either had to allude to and build on the known connotations of the birds or to counteract them before he could have the freedom to establish a new identity for each. This animal lore comprised a et of assumptions, beliefs, and interpretations, sometimes conflicting, derived from different sources. These sources can be classified roughly as bestiaries, beast fables, encyclopaedic works on natural history, together with Isidore of Seville's book of etymologies, and certain classical writings, in particular Ovid's *Metamorphoses*.

The traditions of the nightingale were predominantly favourable; those of the owl on the whole unfavourable; but there were several different traditions for each bird.[5] The nightingale, according to the courtly love tradition, was a bird who sang of joy and of spring. The contrary idea, deriving ultimately from the story of the rape of Philomena, that the nightingale's song was one of lament and even death, is not alluded to in *The Owl and the Nightingale*. In lyrics the nightingale is the bird who sings of love in spring. The notion of the nightingale as a symbol of the amorous kind of courtly love was taken further, probably owing to the fable of the nightingale whose song formed the link between a man and his married lover (alluded to in lines 1049-62), whereby the nightingale became,

---

[4] A contrary view to the opinion supported and developed in this essay, that the poem is essentially about discord, is put forward by Brian Stone in the introduction to his translation (1971:155-80). He sees it rather as "... a complex interpretation of important comtemporary ideas ... a whole philosophy of life emerges from the conflict, a charitable, pragmatic and ... humanistic system of values superior to that inherent in either of the formal positions taken up by the two birds" (1971:155-6). According to him the reader is forced "... to concentrate on the intellectual and moral issues raised, in an atmosphere made sane by laughter" (1971:180). While there is clearly something in this view, for the poet does take the ideas seriously, his mockery of the birds has pride of place and must surely be central to any interpretation.

[5] For summaries of the bird lore of each bird from classical times to today, see Rowland (1978:105-11, 115-20). A more extended account of the nightingale tradition in Christian Latin literature is given by Raby (1951:435-48). A fuller account of the owl can be found in Schwarz and Plagemann, s.v. "Eule" (n.d.: vi.267-322).

in some contexts, a symbol of adultery. The beauty of her song, sur-
passing all musical instruments, along with Isidore's etymology of
the nightingale's name *luscina* as the "singer heralding the light of
dawn", made the way open for a more spiritual view of the bird. In a
tenth-century Latin beast epic, *Escape of a Certain Captive*, the
nightingale sings of Christ's passion and the joys of eternal bliss
(Zeydel, 1964). Just later than the date of *The Owl and the Nightingale*, in two Anglo-Latin poems of the mid-thirteenth century, the
nightingale sings of mystical love and joy and is portrayed as a type
of devout human soul.[6] Except for the lament tradition the author of
The Owl and the Nightingale draws on all the assumptions about the
nightingale familiar from its lore, of lust, love, joy, and spiritual
longing.

The owl was by reputation a more ignoble bird. In one classical tradition she was a bird of darkness with a hateful voice,
haunting sepulchres, a sign of woe and death. The owl was also an
attribute of Minerva, the goddess of wisdom, from which the Christian fathers reinterpreted the bird as a symbol of idolatry represent-
ing the useless wisdom of the heathen faith. Most bestiaries took the
owl to be a symbol of the Jews dwelling in darkness and avoiding the
true faith, while the small birds who mobbed the owl represented
Christian souls. A more favourable view of the owl to be found in
some bestiaries looks on the bird as Christ seeking out man's soul in
the darkness of his sin. For the owl, just as for the nightingale, the
author of *The Owl and the Nightingale* appears to call upon all the
traditions, omitting only the one specific link with the Jews.

On beginning the poem, then, the medieval reader or listener
would have come with assumptions about the nightingale that were
favourable and, since the pejorative view predominated, expectations
of meeting an evil owl. Yet, from the outset, we see that these clear-
cut expectations will not be fulfilled. Both birds are bursting with
rage and malice, and the nightingale in particular, perched as she is
in the green and flowering thicket, singing more beautifully than
musical instruments, jars with this conventionally delightful setting
when she begins to berate the owl with such rancour. Later we will
see the nightingale laying claim to her traditional role of bringer of
joy, hope, love, and mystical yearning. But her behaviour on first
acquaintance belies her good reputation. The beautiful song turns out

[6] *Philomena* by John of Howden (d. c.1278) and *Philomena praevia temporis
amoeni* by John Pecham (d. 1292); see Raby (1951).

to be a vicious verbal assault on the owl which, while it may help to
define our approach to the owl, at the same time reflects on the character of the nightingale. What the nightingale has to say about the
owl's habits, appearance, and ugly voice confirms at a very superficial level our expectations about that bird's evil nature. But however appropriately used of the owl the word "foul" coming four
times in the lines (ll.31-40), and another seven times not far on
(ll.87-104), and in two further lines again (ll.124 and 130), inter-
spersed with "loth / loathly" in ll.32, 71, 72, 91, and 115, from the
nightingale's mouth cannot but detract from the nightingale herself,
depicting her as more a bird of fate than a bird of love.

A similar rebound effect is achieved at a later point with the
owl. The owl's portrayal as a repulsive bad-tempered creature does
not contradict expectations in the same way as the nightingale's
portrayal does, but as the debate goes on the owl pretends to sterner
moral stuff than the nightingale. She strongly condemns the spring-
time sexual activities of both men and animals, naming specifically
the nightingale. Yet, the terms in which she denounces lechery in no
less than thirty-six lines (ll.487-522) despite her sanctimonious posture, betray a distinctly prurient mind, which reveals itself again in
her remarks about the privy (ll.591-6).

So the reader comes to the poem with expectations based on
the bird lore which at the very start have to be adjusted, and
throughout the poem reassessed. The debate begins, though, by
dealing with much more mundane and realistically bird-like qualities
than any ideas which the owl or the nightingale might symbolise.
This in itself dispels any lofty notions about the birds which their
lore might suggest. The birds open their dispute with attacks on one
another's appearance and habits, which as debating points are paltry
quibbles, and which the low level of argument does nothing to
redeem. At this stage the charges made by the birds are so subjective
and emotional as almost to preclude rational argument. Charges such
as the nightingale makes against the owl of unnaturalness, ugliness,
uncleanness, and the so-called vices of large size, strength, and shun-
ning the light would in any case be hard to refute by logic. Nevertheless the birds profess to be arguing with reason and genuinely
seeking the truth.

In structure the debate moves from the trivial to the serious.
The birds attack one another first about the superficial qualities of
their appearance, habits, and song. This clash leads to claims by the
birds about their practical worth, that is to say their usefulness, and

then to arguments about their moral worth, and finally to assertions about their spiritual value to man. All this sounds very important, and one would expect that the weightier the subject taken up the deeper the treatment would become. But the conduct of the argument, in which character defamation takes precedence over logical reasoning and the contestants want to win at all costs rather than to seek the truth as they claim to be doing, continually debases the affair, however sound some of the points the birds make may be. For instance, the owl betrays a greater interest in vengeance than in truth when she says *Ich wille bon of þe awreke; / & lust hu ich con me bitelle / Mid riȝte soþe witute spelle* (ll.262-4; 'I will be avenged on you; and listen to how I can defend myself with straightforward truth without circumlocution'). Although many cogent points are made in the course of the debate relating to rival views about central issues of the day, as when the nightingale maintains that man should look heavenward with joy while the owl urges that he should weep for his sins, the birds themselves as champions of one or other view do nothing but undermine their own position.

Their masquerade as bold warriors is a case in point. The illustrations the birds hope to impress us with are either inappropriate or they misfire. Can we take seriously a nightingale who, from her safe thicket, thinks she has courage enough to face a wild boar (ll.407-8)? Is the owl who follows soldiers on their campaigns not more of an image of death than of valour (ll.385-90)? She hardly cuts a heroic figure, either, by comparing herself to a hare (ll.373-84). Moreover her choice of the hare, which is a familiar symbol of fecundity and lust, does little to advance her cause against the nightingale whom she castigates later for inciting amorous love.

There are several debating strategies which the birds use in conducting their verbal battle, and the way they handle these strategies is riddled with flaws. Sometimes a point is acknowledged and poorly answered; a fault may be tacitly defended through an attack on its contrary; a weakness may be acclaimed as a virtue; a point may be denied without argument; or the defender may denounce the identical vice in the other bird.

A point acknowledged by the owl is her night flying. But she presents a very weak case for its defence. She professes to be safeguarding from her talons the small birds who would mob her in the day (ll.265-308). For one thing this is clearly not true. As the poet later reveals (ll. 1707-9) she is, in fact, afraid. For another, the owl is now using as a defence one of the very points for which she disparaged the nightingale (ll.150-51), that she would not fly out of her protective cover.

Turning the tables on the opponent with an attack on the contrary quality we see in the owl's response to the charge of size and strength. The owl scoffs at the nightingale for her puny frame with ... *þu nart strong, / Ne þu nart picke, ne þu nart long* (ll.579-80; 'you are not strong, you are not stout, you are not at tall').

The proud adoption as a virtue of the quality attacked we find in the nightingale's answer to the charge of physical weakness. With ingenious sophistry she takes "strength" to include mental powers. Her "strength", she says, is cunning, which can always conquer brute force (ll.755-60).

A point denied by the owl is having an ugly song. In trying to counter this attack in all ways at once the owl succeeds in one. Her voice, she retorts, *is* melodious. It is loud and strong like the great hunting horn. But we can hardly accept this as emitting such mellifluous notes as the harp or pipe, instruments rivalled by the nightingale's song. Then, from her doubtful premise, the owl resoundingly concludes *Ich singe bet þan þu dest* (l.321; 'I sing better than you do'). Yet, as if aware of her weak position in calling the nightingale's song "thin chatter" she quickly shifts ground. However beautiful the nightingale's voice might be, she says, it palls through excess.

The method of attacking the same quality as the indictment, like a game of tit for tat, is used with particular ineptitude by the owl over the matter of uncleanness. She censures the nightingale for uncleanness too, and defends herself against the charge in two incompatible ways, by both justifying and denying it. She accuses the nightingale of choosing an unclean site for her nest, which is, of course, a habitat natural to the bird. At the same time she claims that the uncleanness of her own young in fouling their nest is perfectly natural and right. But then, with brazen inconsistency, she explains that the shape of her nest ensures that it is not fouled at all.

Another way of imputing the same fault to the other bird is to call it by a different name, using a euphemism, as the nightingale does for deception. The tricks of the owl she calls "treachery", those of herself "clever cunning".

When the dispute moves on from natural qualities to include philosophical and religious topics, the birds' debating incompetence persists. They shift ground, they change definitions, they make contradictory points, and they tell lies, all in an attempt to gain su-

premacy at all costs. The nightingale may be more slippery and the
owl more blunt in keeping with their physical powers, but for scant
clarity of thought and poor command of logic there is little to choose
between them. This does not mean that the discussions want interest,
or that they lack valid points. They certainly present various views
current about important topics for the reader's appraisal, but not in a
way which reveals the author as partisan on any of the subjects, and
still less as siding with one or other bird. When the nightingale
thinks that the owl has won the round of uncleanliness and would
now have to fight "against truth and justice" (l. 668), we cannot
agree with her. Nor can we concur with the way the owl judges the
nightingale's long speech with "she spoke well at first, and came to
grief at the end" (ll.1512-4), when in fact it begins with a defence of
love and ends with a condemnation of adultery.

The styles of argument conducted by the birds and their characters are established in the context of their natural qualities. Compared with animals in bestiaries and most beast fables, these two
birds are very naturalistic. They are unmistakably an owl and a
nightingale. One cannot forget that they live in the wood on the
periphery of the human world, that they nest, hatch eggs, catch prey,
sing, and fly. Their normal animal characteristics do not square with
their inflated notions of their worth, and this incongruity at once
diminishes their stature and displays the birds as objects of satire. It
also gave the poet scope to make original use of the bird lore as an
important contribution to his treatment of his theme of human
contentiousness.

As the poem develops the bird lore which regards the birds as
signs to men or symbols, comes more and more into focus and provides the impetus for much of the dispute. Neither bird simply tries
to uphold the *in bono* meaning for itself and the *in malo* meaning for
the other, but, as is typical of their immature notion of debate, they
try to accommodate every quality to their own posture of virtue.

Take the question of love. The owl selects the most unfavourable aspect of the lore of the nightingale and accuses her of inciting
women to lust and encouraging general wantonness. The nightingale,
while denying the specific charge of causing lechery, is nevertheless
prepared to excuse the vice in maidens and her own role in arousing
it. She also lays claim to incompatible traditions of her song of love,
asserting that she sings of both secular and mystical love. On secular
love she is equally contradictory for her song, she says, reflects the
joyous love of a virtuous wife for her husband, and at the same time,

by its brevity, it teaches young girls how transitory love is. This is at odds again with her assertion that by its beauty her song reminds man of things eternal. For the owl there was no lore of love, but her gloom and doom reputation makes her condemn the joys and speak only of unhappy wives with cruel husbands. As a corollary to this she goes on to condone adultery by ill-treated wives, a view which undermines her pompous moral stand on lust. Even stranger, she appears to hope for the tyrant's death, as the remark *An for heom bidde Cristis ore, / Þa þe lauedi sone aredde / An hire sende betere ibedde* (ll. 1568-70; 'And for them I pray for Christ's mercy that he will soon rescue the lady and send her a better bed-fellow'), seems to imply. This is a somewhat questionable remedy, eroding still further the owl's self-righteous pose.

Thus both birds take a distinctly dubious moral stance on lust and adultery. The nightingale may be right that in condemning wantonness, a sin of the flesh, one might be prompted by the greater sin of pride, a sin of the spirit, by this clearly does not justify the lesser sin or the excuses made for it. The fallacious views of the birds on this question, which is theologically clear-cut, reduce the credibility of all their other ideas and make their pretensions of conferring spiritual benefits on mankind highly suspect.

A more problematic philosophical question, the matter of foreknowledge, gets extensive treatment by these argumentative birds with their unreliable opinions and evasive ways. Here again the poet draws on bird lore and has each bird trying to turn it to her own advantage. The nightingale puts the owl's reputation for prophecy in the worst possible light. The power brings misery by foretelling disaster while being useless in preventing it. It is a kind of witchcraft, the nightingale claims. A hint of the owl's link with pagan practices had been made very early on when the nightingale taunted the owl about her eyes which looked "just as if they were painted with woad" (l.76). And now (ll.1325-30), by comparing the owl with her astrology to an ape, a familiar image of the devil, and frequently put with the owl to pair the worst animal with the worst bird, the nightingale is denouncing the owl not simply as an ordinary ill-doer but as an apostate.

These two major topics in the poem, adultery and prophecy, give rise to the two violent incidents that are thrown up in the debate, the deaths of the birds, which they each try to suggest on their own behalf are some kind of redemptive sacrifice. Some critics take these two deaths as keys to the meaning of the poem, that the owl as a scarecrow is, in fact, here a symbol of Christ crucified, and that the nightingale torn apart by wild horses in the fable (l.1062) is, in this poem, a symbol of lust. But neither symbolic value can be upheld. Both ideas draw on bird lore, yet this, as we have seen, can never be taken at its face value in this poem since it is always part of the birds' specious arguing. According to the nightingale the scarecrow owl is pelted with sticks through hatred and fear of her prophecies. Together with the repellent description of the scarecrow (ll. 1111-38) this cancels out the owl's presumptuous allusion to Christ's sacrifice. Any possible sparks of divinity which we might want to detect in this ill-tempered bird have already been extinguished by the frequent comparisons of the owl with a worthless, churlish, or wicked man during the course of the poem. Yet the nightingale's presentation of a wholly evil owl cannot be sustained in full either, owing to the owl's undeniable usefulness to man. Equally the nightingale's ludicrously grandiose notion that her death brought some kind of salvation can be discounted. If practical, moral, or spiritual value to man are the criteria, then the nightingale's death was irrelevant, even though it was said to protect the race of nightingales thereafter. The owl, of course, picks on the pejorative connotation of the nightingale's death as being the just deserts of seduction. And again this extreme verdict id redressed by the beneficial effect the nightingale's death had in bringing the jealous knight to justice.

It is clear then that the symbolic values of the deaths deriving from the lore carry no weight in this poem. The quarrelsome nature of the birds, which has already annulled their traditional meaning in relation to other topics, sees to that. Their irrational pugnacity has set the discordant tone throughout, and we can agree with Kathryn Hume that the deaths serve together as an image of the destructive consequences of hate. They are an inevitable and pointless by-product of the quarrel rather than its direct result, for it is not the issues which count here, it is the squabble itself.

As Hume puts it (1975:100), the deaths show:

> ... the evil results of quarrelling. The grim spirit of altercation often demands the death of one contestant. Man kills because that is part of quarrelling, even when he gains nothing from the birds' deaths. Disasters are not warded off by crucifying the Owl, or adultery by dismembering the Nightingale. I interpret the birds' slaughter simply as an object lesson on the results of

quarrelling, proof of the evils inherent in contentiousness.

The debate, then, satirises the vice of contentiousness by mocking its
stupidity in the bellicose birds and their inability to tackle any of the
topics with clarity or sense, and despite the comic effects of the satire
the poem does not deny the serious consequences of this vice.
Finding ourselves ... *in some sumere dale; / on one supe diȝele hale*
(ll.1-2; 'in a summery valley in a very secluded nook'), we are
surprised at the discordant tone when we first meet the birds who ...
*aiper aȝen oper sval / & let pat voole mod ut al; / & eiper seide of
operes custe / pat alre worste pat hi wuste* (ll.7-10; 'each swelled up
in rage at the other and let all these offensive thoughts burst out, and
each said about the other's character the very worst things that she
knew'). We are shocked near the end of the poem by the violent
deaths described of a nightingale and an owl. After the attacks and
counter-attacks, the sophistry and abuse, the task of Nicholas of
Guildford will not be to judge the issues nor to decide between the
contending parties but to act as keeper of the peace.
     The one redeeming feature possessed by both birds is their
willingness to submit to judgment. even if their preference for legal
arbitration to open combat stems from their fear, for as we have
seen they are both, in fact, afraid to fight, this does not discredit the
value of peace. On the contrary, the fact that they agree to be judged
by Nicholas of Guildford is the one stable factor of the poem. The
birds remind one another of their pledge (ll.541-55, 1689-96), and
the wren, wise king of the birds, urges them to keep it (ll.1733-8).
We see that the birds will have to relinquish their quarrel, since it
has been shown up as baseless folly, and be reconciled. Their angry
feeling will have to give way to the higher demands of truth, reason
and harmony.
     As they move off to Portesham the owl and the nightingale
emerge at last from cover and meet each other alone in the open.
Agreeing about how to present their case, they at last display mutual
trust:

> "Do we," þe Niȝtegale seide;
> "Ah wa schal unker speche rede,
> An telle touore unker deme?"
>   "Þarof ich schal þe wel icweme,"
> Cwaþ þe Houle, "for al, ende of orde,

Telle ich con, word after worde.
An ȝef þe þincþ þat ich misrempe
Þu stond aȝein & do me crempe."
Mid þisse worde forþ hi ferden,
Al bute here & bute uerde,
To Portesham þat heo bicome.   (1781-91)

("Enough," said the Nightingale, "but who shall bring forward our pleas and tell them in front of our judge?" "I will please you in this matter," said the Owl, "since I can tell everything word for word from the beginning to the end. And if you think that I am going astray, you must stand up against me and restrain me." With these words they went off, without any army and without any troops, to Portesham, and there they arrived.)

This conciliatory act and the preferment they hope to accomplish for Nicholas of Guildford are, after the stormy passage of the poem, final affirmations of the value of peace.

REFERENCES

Hume, Kathryn (1975). *The Owl and the Nightingale: The Poem and its Critics.* Toronto: University of Toronto Press.
Lumiansky, R.M. (1953). Concerning *The Owl and the Nightingale. Philological Quarterly* 32. 411-17.
Raby, F.J.E. (1951). *Philomena praevia temporis amoeni.* In: *Mélanges Joseph de Ghellinck, S.J.* Tome II: "Moyen Age". Gembloux.
Rowland, Beryl (1978). *Birds with Human Souls: A Guide to Bird Symbolism.* Knoxville, TN: University of Tennessee Press.
Schwarz, H. and V. Plagemann (n.d.). *Reallexicon zur deutschen Kunstgeschichte.*
Stanley, E.G. (ed.) (1960). *The Owl and the Nightingale.* London and Edinburgh: Nelson. (Repr. 1972. Manchester: Manchester University Press.).
Stone, Brian (trans.) (1971). *The Owl and the Nightingale, Cleanness, St Erkenwald.* Penguin Classics. Harmondsworth, Middlesex: Penguin Books.
Utley, F.L. (1972). The Owl and the Nightingale. In: *A Manual of Writings in Middle English.* Ed. A.E. Hartung. Vol.3. New Haven, CT: The Connecticut Academy of Arts and Sciences. 716-20, 874-82.
Zeydel, Edwin H. (ed. and trans.) (1964). *Ecsbasis cuiusdam captivi per tropologiam: Escape of a Certain Captive told in a Figurative Manner.* Chapel Hill, NC: University of North Carolina Press.

THE TWOFOLD HARMONY
OF
THE MIDDLE ENGLISH *SIR ORFEO*

ERIK KOOPER
(University of Utrecht)

On a nice and sunny morning in May when the orchard was blos-
soming and there were flowers everywhere Dame Heurodis, wife to
Orfeo, the king of Traciens, fell asleep under a tree in her garden. In
spite of the pleasant entourage she had a nightmare in which the king
of fairies ordered her to be under the same tree the next day because
he wanted to take her with him to his kingdom. Naturally Sir Orfeo
took all the precautions he could think of: he placed his wife in the
middle of a cordon of "ten hundred" heavily armoured knights, each
and all willing to die in defence of their queen. But as if this
"scheltrom" never existed, the king of the Other World carried her
off just like that: *Ac ʒete amiddes hem ful riʒt / Þe quen was oway
ytviʒt, / ... Men wiste neuer wher sche was bicome* (ll.191-4: 'But
yet from their midst, straightaway, the queen was snatched away, ...
They did not know at all where she had gone').[1] As a result her
husband suffered a mental breakdown, and at a meeting of his
baronial council Orfeo announced that he would leave his kingdom
in the hands of his trusted steward *To kepe [his] londes oueral*
(l.208), because the loss of his wife had made him decide to retire to
the wilderness to *liue per euermore / Wiþ wilde bestes in holtes hore*
(ll.213-14: 'to live there for ever among the wild animals in the grey
woods'). Should they hear that he has died, then they must convene a
parliament and choose themselves a new king. He refused to be
mollified by the entreaties of his nobles, and dressed in a simple
pilgrim's robe Orfeo entered into his voluntary exile, taking with
him only his harp.

---

[1] All quotations are from the Auchinleck text as printed in Bliss (1954), including
the reconstructed opening lines, but with a few adaptations (e.g. *and* for *&*). For a
well-argued defence of the use of the Auchinleck redaction, see Lerer (1985:94).

At this point in the poem all the signs are that we have reached the end not merely of Orfeo's marriage and reign, but possibly even of his kingdom, weakened as it seems by the collapse of its undisputed, popular ruler. At this point, too, it must have become clear to the audience that they were being presented with a version of the well-known story of Orpheus and Eurydice, into which the poet introduced a number of new elements, for instance Orfeo not only as husband to Heurodis but also as king and ruler, and the Fairy King and his Other World. This paper is an attempt to answer a few questions connected with these changes, the most obvious one being why the poet deviated from the classical tale by adding a happy reunion of Orfeo with Heurodis, as well as Orfeo's recovery of his kingdom. The questions are not easy and finding an answer to them will involve, among other things, a study of medieval political theories concerning rulership. Moreover, a solution will only be acceptable if it is to leave room for an explanation of the function of the harp.

As a narrative and a poem *Sir Orfeo* has been widely praised by the critics. Its editor, Bliss, thought of it as "an outstanding example of narrative skill" (1954:xli). The poet's artistry shows in the suspense he is building up, for example when he has us wait for over fifty lines before revealing the contents of Heurodis' nightmare (for more instances, see Burke Severs, 1961:201). The poetic quality of the poem has been commented upon by, among others, Lerer (1985), and concrete examples illustrating it are not difficult to find: when Heurodis is first introduced to us we are told that she is the most beautiful lady of all, but no more:

> Þe king hadde a quen of priis
> Þat was ycleped Dame Heurodis,
> Þe fairest leuedi, for þe nones,
> Þat miȝt gon on bodi and bones,
> Ful of loue and of godenisse;
> Ac no man may telle hir fairnisse.   (51-6)

(The king had a queen of excellence who was called Lady Heurodis, truly the prettiest lady that might exist, full of love and goodness; no one indeed can describe her beauty.)

The indescribability topos is no more than a poetic device, for a fuller description is soon to follow. After her nightmare, Heurodis is brought inside and put to bed, while Orfeo is being warned. When he arrives we see Heurodis through his eyes and we are horrified with him: her body, her fingers, her eyes, the colour of her face, all exponents of true feminine beauty, have been turned into their gruesome opposites. What we see is beauty destroyed:

> "Þi bodi, þat was so white ycore,
> Wiþ þine nailes is al totore.
> Allas! þi rode, þat was so red,
> Is al wan, as þou were ded;
> And also þine fingres smale
> Beþ al blodi and al pale.
> Allas! þi louesom eyзen to
> Lokeþ so man doþ on his fo!"   (105-12)

("Your body, which was so beautifully white, has all been rent by your nails. Alas! The colour of your face, which was so red, is all wan, as if you were dead; And also your delicate fingers are all bloody and pale. Alas! Your two lovely eyes look as those of one looking at his enemy!")

If the poetic and narrative qualities of *Sir Orfeo* are beyond doubt, its structure and its main concerns are still subject of critical debate. Thus Mortimer J. Donovan praises the lay as a unified poem of great beauty, told with "a care marred, if at all, in one way only: Orfeo's return and recognition draws attention from Heurodis' rescue and homecoming, which should be the climax of the poem" (1967:136). Donovan here refers to a concern shared by many critics who have difficulty in seeing *Sir Orfeo* detached from its classical original, and which was worded by David Lyle Jeffrey as follows: "Why, among all versions of the story, should the 'skillful narrator' of this fourteenth-century tale of faërie so deliberately distort the obvious psychological high point of his story?" (1976:45). This is indeed a question that keeps nagging critics;[2] it will be my purpose in this article to show that both the reunion of Orfeo and Heurodis and the homecoming scene are of crucial importance to at least one major theme of the poem, that of ideal kingship.[3]

---

[2] Some critics ask the question but do not answer it (e.g. Jeffrey, 1976: 45, 58).

[3] Critics have also defended the inclusion of the final episode on such grounds as structural balance (Bliss, 1954:xliii), the unity of narrative technique (suspense) and the parallels between the two "climactic episodes—recovery of Heurodis and recovery of kingdom" (Burke Severs, 1961:201-2), or "human interest and the

In a paper published in 1961, D. M. Hill argued that *Sir Orfeo* consists of three parts:[4] a short introduction and two sections containing the two "assays," as he calls them, of the poem. About these he says: "The major assay concerns the testing of Orfeo and Heurodis and through them the quality of human heterosexual ... love. The minor assay concerns the testing of the steward and through him the quality of male ... love" (1961:139). The type first mentioned is the new kind of love, the subject of romances, the second the old, epic type. Hill concludes: "The poet of *Sir Orfeo* [maintains] that 'romance' love and 'epic' love differ in importance: the former is greater than the latter which depends on it. If A, then B" (1961:149). If I interpret Hill correctly, he sees as the poem's main theme the weighting of these two types of love, 'epic' and 'romance' love. I think that he is right to the extent that the testing of the love between, on the one hand, Orfeo and Heurodis, and, on the other, Orfeo and his steward, is an essential feature of the poem. But *Sir Orfeo* is about more than just that.

A most important contribution to the poem's interpretion is an article by Peter Lucas, which appeared in 1972. He also focuses his attention on the two "assays"; however, he differs from Hill in considering these not as the testing of two relationships based on love, but as a trial of the two essential bonds of society, "private, reciprocal marital love and its corollary, public loyalty" (1972:8).[5]

I can go along with most of what Lucas says, but his suggestion leaves open the question whether, and, if so, when, these two bonds indeed constituted the basic social relationships. Apart from that he stresses the importance of the harp, but foregoes to pay any attention to its, possibly symbolic, meaning.

In what follows I intend to look briefly into medieval theories about kingship to see how they relate to the poem, and at the function of the harp in the narrative; I shall suggest that there is a connection between this function and that of the king.

---

imposition of a consistent moral pattern" (Kinghorn, 1950:362). The only one to have considered "the relationship between the personal desires and feelings of the king and his role as ruler" is A.S.G. Edwards (1981:283).

[4] Bliss (1954:xli) suggests four sections and Burke Severs (1961:199) four and a prologue (Prol. 1-56; I. 57-194; II. 195-280; III. 281-476; IV. 477-605).

[5] This comes very close to the approach taken by Edwards (1981), but was apparently overlooked by the latter.

Further consideration of Lucas's suggestion that Orfeo partakes in two bonds of society leads us to assume a threefold division of that society: the individual citizen, the household and the state. This is typically an Aristotelian concept and is found in the *Ethics* and the *Politics*. The impact of these two books can clearly be seen in the works of Thomas Aquinas and another important political theorist, a pupil of Thomas, Giles of Rome (also known as Aegidius Romanus, Egidio Colonna or Gilles de Rome). Between 1260 and 1270 Thomas wrote a commentary on the *Ethics*; he has also left us an incomplete commentary on the *Politics*, but his *Summa Theologiae* shows beyond doubt that he was well acquainted with both works in their entirety. Giles of Rome (d. 1316) produced his *De regimine principum* a little later (1284-5), at the request of Philip the Fair, whose tutor he was, and who in 1286 ordered Henri de Gauchi to translate the work into French. Translations in other vernaculars followed; that in English, usually ascribed to John Trevisa, about a hundred years later.[6] His work follows, says Minnis (1983:73), "the Aristotelian division of practical philosophy into ethics, economics and politics." Ethics teaches the prince how to rule himself, economics how to rule his wife and politics how to govern a state. This tripartite division, together with the headings here given, is used by Gower in Book VII of his *Confessio Amantis*, which deals with the education of a king.[7] In a paper on the influence of Giles on Gower, Elizabeth Porter gives a useful summary of the basic tenets of his *De regimine*, the gist of which is the following:

> Giles begins his treatise with a systematic exposition of the individual's need to acquire ethical self-governance, or personal kingship. Although his work is designed as a 'mirror for princes' he stresses here, as throughout his treatise, that his instruction is useful to everyone. For although not everyone is able to be a king or a prince everyone ought to strive to be such that he may be worthy to rule. This personal kingship ... is not an end in itself but is related by Giles to man's need to live as part of a community, ... for it is only as part of a com-

6 The text has never been edited, but an edition by David Fowler and Charles Briggs is forthcoming. Childs gives a summary of the text and transcriptions of a number of passages (1932:46-68, 182-314).

7 For a more extensive exposition of these ideas, see Kooper (1991:146-8).

munity that [his] complex needs may be met and [his]
highest good, which is the pursuit of wisdom and virtue,
may be exercised. ...

   Ethical self-governance, therefore, enables men to
contribute to their communities, both the small community of the family and the large community of the body
politic. In Giles' view the second is more perfect than
the first, since ... marriage and the establishment of a
family is seen as a miniature image of the political community of the state [while] the well-being of the state
will depend on [the] well-regulated households for, as
Giles argues, the political community is made up of an
infinite number of such families.   (Porter, 1983: 139)

The three layers of society meet in the king, who consequently must
fulfil a model function for correct behaviour in all three divisions.
But a chain is only as strong as its weakest link, and therefore it is
the additional duty of the king to make it his personal responsibility
that all his subjects, i.e. every member of the larger community, feel
so much at ease that such behaviour can be developed.
   In the opening passage of *Sir Orfeo* we see Orfeo in this very
role:

   Orfeo mest of ani þing
   Loued þe gle of harping;
   Siker was eueri gode harpour
   Of him to haue miche honour.
   Himself he lerned forto harp,
   And leyd þeron his wittes scharp;
   He lerned so, þer noþing was
   A better harpour in no plas.
   In al þe warld was no man bore
   Þat ones Orfeo sat bifore
   (And he miȝt of his harping here)
   Bot he schuld þenche þat he were
   In on of þe ioies of Paradis,
   Swiche melody in his harping is.   (25-38)

(More than anything else Orfeo loved the minstrelsy of playing the
harp; every good harpist could certainly expect to be much honoured
by him. He himself learned to play the harp and set his sharp mind
to it. He learned it so well that there was not a better harpist any-

where at all. In all the world there was no born man who, once he
sat before Orfeo and might hear his harping, did not think that he
was enjoying the joys of Paradise—such beautiful melody there is in
his harp playing.)

As an explanation it would be insufficient to say that the
thorough enjoyment of the music makes the listener feel himself in
paradise. A more fundamental concept is underlyng these lines, symbolized by Orfeo's harp.

In his extensive monograph on the figure of Orpheus in the
Middle Ages, John Friedman has presented evidence that from a very
early period onwards (at least from the sixth century) Orpheus had
been associated with David (1970:148; cf. also Jeffrey, 1976:50-4).
Both were kings, both were harpists, and, as the *Glossa ordinaria*
explains:

> David was skilled in song (*canticus musicae*); so, as it
> were, by the sweetness of the harp of speech (*citharae
> locutionis*) our peace of mind (*tranquilitate*) is restored.
> Saul was (thereby) refreshed, (whereas) before he was
> truly tormented by the devil almost to the point of suf-
> focation.[8]

The harp is traditionally the instrument that symbolizes harmony,
and medieval biblical commentators interpret the power of David's
music as an ability to (re)order the microcosmos: by means of the
music of the harp the distorted harmony between the soul and the
body of Saul can be restored (Van Schaik, 1988:38-41). Through this
faculty David is associated with Christ. However, the opening
passage of *Sir Orfeo*, in which Orfeo's skill as a harp player is presented in great detail, has no explicit references to David or Christ,
nor is the poem as a whole so Christian that an identification of
Orfeo as either of them is forced upon us.[9] The conclusion must be

---

[8] Quoted from Jeffrey's translation (1976:54) of the text of the *Glossa* in Migne's
Patrologia Latina, 113, cols. 555-6. The same idea is found in an anonymous
fifteenth-century commentary on the *Eclogue* of Theodulus: "Just as Orpheus
played his lyre in hell, so David played before Saul; and just as Orpheus softened
the gods of the underworld with his lyre, so David softened Saul's evil spirit"
(Friedman, 1970:149). It was apparently a medieval commonplace.
[9] As Jeffrey puts it (1976:49): "Why, if Orfeo were Christ (or God), should the
leaving of his throne be carefully described in terms of abdication and abandoned

that an explanation of the function of the harp in the poem should be sought for elsewhere.

In the chapter on music and its enjoyment in his *Policraticus* or *De Nugis Curialum* John of Salisbury, echoing Boethius's *De Musica* (Jeffrey, 1976:55), had said that the music produced by the harp is so powerful that this music, together with its many forms and "the harmonies that serve it, ... embraces the universe," and he goes on (I.vi.39):

> [Music] reconciles the clashing and dissonant relations of all that exists and of all that is thought and expressed in words by a sort of ever varying but still harmonious law derived from its own symmetry. By it the phenomena of the heavens are ruled and the activities of the world and men are governed.[10]   (Pike, 1972:30)

John follows Plato (and common opinion, as he says himself) in thinking that the soul "consists of musical harmonies" (*ex consonantiis musicis esse compositam*—I.vi.40). These harmonies could be disrupted and in such instances superb harpists like David (and Orpheus, we may add) were able to restore them by their music; that is how David soothed the evil spirit in Saul (and how Orpheus charmed Pluto).

Also my last long quotation strikes a distinctly Boethian note. The twelfth century has been called "Boethius's golden age",[11] and the spirit of the *Consolation of Philosophy* is visible in the entire *Policraticus*. In relation to my quotation I may refer to a famous metre in the *Consolation* (II.m.8) where it is said that

---

self-exile (ll. 206-26), or why, if the allegory were reasonably consistent, would he attempt to defend Eurydice with horses and men—and vainly? (ll.175-94)".

[10] "...*uirtutits suae potentia specierumque uarietate et sibi famulantibus numeris uniuersa complectitur, omnium quae sunt et quae dicuntur, dissidentem et dissonam multitudinem proportionum suarum, id est, inaequali quadam aequitatis lege concilians. Hac etenim celestia temperantur, mundana siue humana reguntur.*" All quotations in Latin are from Webb (1965). Dickinson's (1927) partial translation (Books IV, V, VI, VII.xvi-xxi, xxv, and VIII.xvii-xxii) is complemented by that of Pike (1972).

[11] Haring, 1969:287. For a purely Boethian interpretation of *Sir Orfeo*, see Knapp (1968).

all this harmonious order of things is achieved by love
which rules the earth and the seas, and commands the
heavens.[12]

This is the love, *amor*, that binds together human beings in their
various relationships. The metre ends as follows:

Love binds together people joined by a sacred bond;
love binds sacred marriages by chaste affections; love
makes the laws which join true friends. O how happy
the human race would be, if that love [*amor*] which
rules the heavens ruled also your souls.[13]

(Green, 1962:41)

Medieval commentators gloss *amor* as God.[14] Therefore, what these
lines purport to say is: if divine love ruled in the souls of all men,
not only would they themselves enjoy the inner harmony of the soul
of every individual but there would be peace and concord at the
other two levels of society, the household and the state, as well.

In a later metre (III.m.9) we find the same basic principle expressed in slightly different words. Lady Philosophy here explains to
Boethius that man's soul is part of the world-soul (Green's free
translation of *natura*), which God released "throughout the harmonious parts of the universe as [his] surrogate ... to give motion to all
things."[15] She also tells Boethius that the essentially opposing ele-

---

[12] *"Hanc rerum seriem ligat / Terras ac pelagus regens / Et caelo imperitans amor"*
(13-5). Quoted from Tester (1973). All translations are quoted from Green (1962),
here p. 41.

[13]   Hic sancto populos quoque
         Iunctos foedere continet,
         Hic et coniugii sacrum
         Castis nectit amoribus,
         Hic fidis etiam sua
         Dictat iura sodalibus.
         O felix hominum genus,
         Si vestros animos amor
         Quo caelum regitur regat. (22-30)

[14] Cf. the gloss quoted by Haring (1969:299): *"Amor dicitur deus quia res que
propria natura in semetipsis discordant in ipso concordant"* (Amor means God
because things which by their own specific nature are among themselves not in
harmony, are so in him —my transl.).

[15]   Tu triplicis medium naturae cuncta moventem

ments of nature (cold and heat, moist and dry) are joined by God, "who govern[s] the world with eternal reason" (*qui perpetua mundum ratione gubernas*—III.m.9, 1). In other words, God's entire creation is imbued with this *natura* and his reason, and because of that the dissimilar elements can be brought into harmony.

In the *Policraticus* we see this idea translated into musical concepts (I.vi.41):

> Although tone is by no means spirit, it certainly is a type of conveyance of spirit and is the medium of spirit.... When heard in its more delicately uttered strains, it captivates with its beauty even austere minds and by the exhibition of a sort of charming gaiety drives gloom away.[16]   (Pike, 1972:31)

*

Let us now return to the opening passage of the poem. Here Orfeo is presented to us as a model king. This is also where the harp comes in: Orfeo's skill on the harp symbolizes that there is harmony in his soul, that in it reason governs the senses.[17] Because of this inner harmony he can transfer that same concord to his subjects, who then feel as if they have regained the paradisaic state (which they had lost as a result of the first sin, when the senses overruled reason).

The inner harmony of Orfeo reflects not only on the bond with his subjects but on that with his wife as well. No reader of the poem will doubt that the relationship between Orfeo and Heurodis is a happy and harmonious one (cf. Kooper, 1990:185-6). Their love is the *amor* of Boethius' *Consolatio* II.m.8, quoted above, or, in the words of Heurodis:

> "Seþþen we first togider were
> Ones wroþ neuer we nere,

Connectens animam per consona membra resolvis. (13-14)
A notoriously difficult passage for which I have followed Green (1962:60).
[16] "*Certe, etsi nulla ratione sit spiritus, eam quoddam uehiculum spiritus esse certissimum est; .... Cum uero modis suis elegantius fuerit colorata, uenustate sui mentes etiam superiores capit, et quadam inductae hilaritatis gratia pellit tristitiam.*"
[17] The harp as a symbol of personal and/or social harmony has been commented upon by many critics, e.g. Jeffrey (1976), Edwards (1981), Lerer (1985), Veldhoen (1990).

> Bot euer ich haue yloued þe
> As mi liif, and so þou me." (121-4)

("Ever since we were first together we have never quarrelled; on the contrary, I have always loved you as my own life, and you me.")

When Orfeo takes his precautions against the expected attempt of the Fairy King to abduct his wife, a thousand armed men go with him and the queen to the *ympe-tree* to protect her:

> Þai made scheltrom in ich a side,
> And sayd þai wold þere abide
> And dye þer euerichon,
> Er þe quen schuld fram hem gon. (187-90)

(They formed a circle of armed men around her, and said that they would stay there and die there, every single one, before the queen should be allowed to leave them.)

These passages show that at the beginning of the poem a situation of harmony exists at all three levels of society, pivoted upon Orfeo. The abduction of Heurodis destroys this harmonious equilibrium. Orfeo is shattered by grief and loses his self-government.

Orfeo now takes a remarkable decision: he appoints a steward and retires to the wilderness. Why should he do that? To answer this we must go back to John of Salisbury and Boethius. In the *Policraticus* we read that the king was to the state as the head to the body, and that the members of the body "will function properly as long as they follow the guidance of the head, and the head remains sane" (IV.i). Beside this John had said that the king should always put the interests of the commonwealth before his private ones. Orfeo's behaviour after the nightmare, and even more so after the abduction, shows that he had lost his self-governance, in other words, that the head of the state was no longer completely *compos mentis*. Only one conclusion is now open to Orfeo: he must appoint a deputy and retire before the state will be affected also (cf. Edwards, 1981:284-5). Is it possible for a king thus to retire without damage to the state? It seems it is: in his *Confessio Amantis* Gower relates the story of the model king Lycurgus "whose laws were so true and well understood that he could remove himself personally from [Athens]" (Peck, 1978:148).

As Burke Severs already observed (although many critics have overlooked this point), Orfeo does not leave his kingdom in order to seek Heurodis, and he continues: "On the contrary, [it] is entirely an unreasoning expression of unbounded grief and overwhelming anguish of spirit. ... He has no plan. He is not going anywhere" (1961: 207; cf. Edwards, 1981:286). A voluntary self-exile into the wilderness also occurs elsewhere in medieval literature, for instance in Chrétien de Troyes' *Yvain* (Hill, 1961:148). As in the case of Yvain, the madness ensuing from Orfeo's emotional shock has at first a devastating impact, but eventually leads to his complete recovery. As Lerer puts it: "... the willing isolation of the hero from society ... helps him to come to terms with himself apart from the demands of feudal and marital life" (1985:98). In the opinion of John of Salisbury (*Policraticus* VII.ii.96) man becomes like a beast, or indeed inferior to a beast, when he loses the powers of discrimination and understanding. The description of Orfeo as a "wild man" depicts him as living like an animal, without the comfort even of the three so-called *temporalia*, food, clothing, housing (238-60), and with his harp hidden in a hollow tree (267-8). Only gradually do we see Orfeo recover, and when the weather is fine and he feels well, he occasionally takes out his harp to play, a little.[18] But his full recovery to a sound and rational man we do not witness until at the court of the Fairy King, where he *tunes* his harp before he begins to play. In the wilderness, when he played just for himself and just as he felt, there was no need to do so, but in this court he can be successful only if the harmony in his own soul has reached its former perfection, if he has recovered his self-government. The tuning of the harp is symbolic of that and in this context it is interesting to know that David is often depicted in the B-initial at the beginning of the psalms not as playing the harp but as tuning it.[19]

[18] Spearing points out that the "association of music with healing, and especially with the healing of mental disorders, is ... traditional" (1987:80-1; see also Jeffrey, 1976:56). However, unlike Spearing I do not see Orfeo's playing of his harp as causal to but as symbolic of his gradual recuperation.

[19] King David is seen here as a *figura* of Christ the Word, upholding the order of both the micro- and the macrocosmos. Historiated initials with this theme occur from the middle of the twelfth century. A list of manuscripts with a tuning David is given by Van Schaik (1988:58-60).

The Other World of the Fairy King is, at first sight, just like our own if only more brilliant and splendid.[20] But it is a world of outward appearances; the people taken there by the Fairy King look exactly as they had been in this world, but they are no more than physical phenomena, bodies without souls (cf. Ronquist, 1985:104). It is a world of violence in which the harmony of Orfeo's kingdom has no place, and to which visitors do not stray.[21] Hence when Orfeo enters it he is the opposite of "the dead and the taken": he has come of his own initiative, determined to reach his goal, but, although a king, dressed in a poor outfit. In his disguise as a minstrel he is not even recognized as such and has to explain the minstrel's craft (419-34). When he sets himself to play his regained self-governance shows in his music, but eventually he wins back his wife through his verbal skill (Lerer, 1985:105, Liuzza, 1991:280)—another sign of his restored rational powers.

Together with Heurodis, Orfeo returns to Winchester. Here the test of the steward's loyalty opens with a scene in which the harp is the focus of attention. Again Orfeo first tunes it before playing, and although a flock of musicians had just finished their performances, everyone immediately recognizes the superb quality of his music. The steward, demonstrating his naiveté in these matters, thinks the music was produced by the harp rather than by the harpist and asks Orfeo how he came to possess such a splendid instrument. Another scene follows in which Orfeo's verbal skill is essential. After he has ascertained the steward's continued loyalty to him, he reveals his identity by means of a hypothesizing question: what if I were the king and had just tested your

> "... gode wille,
> And ich founde þe þus trewe,
> Þou ne schust it neuer rewe.
> Sikerlich, for loue or ay,
> Þou schust be king after mi day."   (568-72)

("... good will and had found you true in that, you would never have reason to regret it. Certainly, for love or fear, you would be king after my death.")

---

[20] For an extended comparison of the two kingdoms, see Lerer (1985) and Liuzza (1991:179).

[21] For an entirely different view of the place, see Veldhoen (1990:118-19).

These lines evoke a passage in Matthew where Christ says:

> "Who is the trusty servant, the sensible man charged by
> his master to manage his household staff and issue their
> rations at the proper time? Happy who is found at his
> task when his master comes![22] I tell you this: he will be
> in charge of his master's property."   (Matt. 24:45-7)

At the beginning of the poem Orfeo had been associated with
David, and through him with Christ. Here at the end we find another
passage evoking a parallel between Christ and Orfeo. In fact, such
passages recur throughout the poem: the opening section with the
harping Orfeo, the episode in the wilderness as a pseudo-death, followed by a visit to the Other-/Underworld, the release of Heurodis,
and finally the parallel pointed out above. But as already remarked at
the beginning of this paper, there is no reason to think of the poem
as distinctly *Christian*, let alone to identify Orfeo as a figure of
Christ. It rather seems as if the poet refers to a similarity existing
between the roles of Orfeo and Christ: in the same way in which
Christ is responsible for and looks after his flock Orfeo takes care of
those dependent on him. In support of this conclusion I may refer to
the Prologue of John Gower's *Confessio Amantis*, where he gives a
description of the ideal, but pagan, king Arion, another harp player.
It is a description which comes very close to that of king Orfeo:

> Bot wolde god that now were on
> An other such as Arion,
> Which hadde an harpe of such temprure,
> And therto of so good mesure
> He song, that he the bestes wilde
> Made of his note tame and milde,
> ...
> The Hare in pees stod with the Hound;
> And every man upon this ground

---

[22] "*Beatus ille servus quem cum venerit dominus eius invenerit sic facientem*"
(italics mine). Note that the first word of the Psalms, so the word in whose intial
the harp playing David is usually depicted, is also *beatus*: "*Beatus vir qui non abiit
in consilio impiorum et in via peccatorum non stetit et in cathedra pestilentiae non
sedit sed in lege Domini voluntas eius et in lege eius meditabitur die ac nocte*" (Ps.
1:1-2).

Which Arion that time herde,
As wel the lord as the shepherde,
He broghte hem alle in good acord. (Prol. 1053-58, 1061-5)

(But would God that there were now someone just like Arion, who
had a well-tuned harp and in addition to that could sing well, so that
he by his song would make the wild animals tame and gentle, ...
[and] the hare lived in peace with the hound; and every man in this
world who heard Arion at that time, both the lord and the shepherd,
would all be broght to concord.)

*

A minor but not uninteresting point has been left to the end. When
Orfeo retired into the wilderness, he left his kingdom in the hands of
his steward. Why, we might wonder, did he not simply abdicate and
why did he not let his council choose a new king straightaway instead
of asking them to wait until his death? The Middle English poem is
generally assumed to be a translation from an Old French or Anglo-
Norman original, probably written in the second half of the twelfth
century (Bliss, 1954:xl-xli; Donovan, 1967:136). At that time the
works of Aristotle had not yet been translated and those of Thomas
Aquinas or Giles of Rome not been written, and we shall therefore
have to look elsewhere if we want to attempt to relate *Sir Orfeo* to
the political theories on kingship current at the time the presumed
original was composed.

In his book on government and politics in the Middle Ages,
Walter Ullmann has argued that the twelfth century can still be
classified as a period in which theocratic kingship held sway. In this
system the king, by the grace of God, is God's representative on
earth (1966:143). This grace of God was acquired by the royal
unction, which then was still a sacrament (1966:140). Although the
king was formally elected to his elevated office, the people who
elected him could not confer any power on him because the people
were the king's *subjecti*, literally his subjects (1966:130, 145); they
were placed under him just as he himself was placed under God
(1966:128). This meant that there was no formal contract stating
their respective obligations between the king and his people, as there
was in the next century with its feudal kingship; an obliging compact
to act loyally and responsibly, a kind of gentlemen's agreement, was
all there was. Naturally a wise king would listen to any advice his
counsellors might give, but he ruled by the principle of the *voluntas*

principis (1966:123). Because the subjects were placed under the king it was extremely difficult to resist his decisions (1966:131), and because the king had been enthroned by means of a sacramental act it was impossible for the king to abdicate or for his people to depose him. In this system, it will be clear, the household is not given any special status.

A writer who expresses the basic tenets of theocratic kingship is John of Salisbury. whose *Policraticus* was finished in 1159, "the only important political treatise written before western thought had once more become familiar with the Politics of Aristotle" (Dickinson, 1927:xvii). If the original version of *Sir Orfeo* came into being between 1150 and 1200, the concept of theocratic kingship and John's work may well have influenced its author.[23] Such an influence would help explain why Orfeo did not abdicate and went through all the trouble of appointing his steward as his deputy, leaving him with the unenviable task of ruling his kingdom in his absence. By twelfth-century standards Orfeo's 'marriage' with his people could not be resolved but by his death.

The role of the harp in the poem is still an important one, also in the context of the ideas sketched above, as symbol of the degree of self-control or inner harmony of the protagonist. Since, in this function, the harp shows little iconological development between the twelfth and the thirteenth centuries, it cannot be used to make any pronouncements on the date of writing of the poem. On the other hand, Orfeo's behaviour in relation to his abdication seems to point to a date rather earlier than the late thirteenth century—the earliest possible time of composition for the Middle English poem. If this conclusion is acceptable then it provides further support for the assumption of a twelfth-century French original.

---

[23] Edwards (1981) also makes use of the concept of the marriage of the king to his state, but follows a different line of interpretation.

REFERENCES

Aertsen, Henk, and Alasdair A. MacDonald (eds.) (1990). *Companion to Middle English Romance*. Amsterdam: VU University Press.

Bliss, A. J. (ed.) (1954). *Sir Orfeo*. London: Oxford University Press.

Childs, Herbert Ellsworth (1932). *A Study of the Unique Middle English Translation of the De Regimine Principum of Aegidius Romanus (MS. Digby 233)*. Ph.D. diss. University of Washington.

Dickinson, John (trans.) (1927). *The Stateman's Book of John of Salisbury*. New York: Alfred A. Knopf.

Donovan, Mortimer J. (1967). Breton Lays. In: *A Manual of the Writings in Middle English 1050-1500*. Gen. ed. J. Burke Severs. Vol. I. New Haven, CT: The Connecticut Academy of Arts and Sciences, 1967. 133-43.

Edwards, A.S.G. (1981). Marriage, Harping and Kingship: The Unity of *Sir Orfeo*. *American Benedictine Review* 32. 282-91.

Friedman, John Block (1970). *Orpheus in the Middle Ages*. Cambridge, MA: Harvard University Press.

Green, Richard (trans.) (1962). *The Consolation of Philosophy*. Indianapolis/New York: Bobbs-Merrill.

Haring, Nicholas, SAC. (1969). Four Commentaries on the *De Consolatione Philosophiae* in MS Heiligenkreuz 130. *Medieval Studies* 31. 287-316.

Hill, D.M. (1961). The Structure of "Sir Orfeo". *Medieval Studies* 23. 136-53.

Jeffrey, David Lyle (1976). The Exiled King: Sir Orfeo's Harp and the Second Death of Eurydice. *Mosaic* 9. 45-60.

Kinghorn, A.A. (1950). Human Interest in the Middle English *Sir Orfeo*. *Neophilologus* 50. 359-69.

Knapp, James F. (1968). The Meaning of *Sir Orfeo*. *Modern Language Quarterly* 29. 263-73.

Kooper, Erik (1990). Love and Marriage in the Middle English Romances. In: Aertsen and MacDonald, 1990:171-87.

Kooper, Erik (1991). Political Theory and Pastoral Care in the *Second Shepherds' Play*. In: *This Noble Craft.... Proceedings of the Xth Research Symposium of the Dutch and Belgian University Teachers of Old and Middle English and Historical Linguistics, Utrecht, 19-20 January, 1989*. Costerus New Series 80. Ed. Erik Kooper. Amsterdam: Rodopi. 142-51.

Liuzza, Roy Michael (1991). *Sir Orfeo*: sources, traditions, and the poetics of performance. *Journal of Medieval and Renaissance Studies* 21. 269-84.

Lucas, Peter (1972). An Interpretation of *Sir Orfeo*. *Leeds Studies in English* NS 6. 1-9.

Macaulay, G.C. (ed.) (1969). *The English Works of John Gower*. 2 vols. EETS ES 81, 82. London: Oxford University Press. (1st publ. 1900, 1901).

Minnis, A.J. (1983a). 'Moral Gower' and Medieval Literary Theory. In: Minnis, 1983b:50-78.

Minnis, A.J. (ed.) (1983b). *Gower's* Confessio Amantis. *Responses and Reassessments*. Cambridge: Brewer.

Peck, Russell A. (1978). *Kingship and Common Profit in Gower's* Confessio Amantis. Carbondale/Edwardsville, IL: Southern Illinois University Press.

Pike, Joseph B. (trans.) (1972). *Frivolities of Courtiers and Footprints of Philosophers*. New York: Octagon Books. (1st publ. 1938).

Porter, Elizabeth (1983). Gower's Ethical Microcosm and Political Macrocosm. In: Minnis, 1983b:135-62.

Ronquist, E.C. (1985). The Powers of Poetry in *Sir Orfeo*. *Philological Quarterly* 64. 99-117.

Severs, J. Burke (1961). The Antecedents of Sir Orfeo. In: *Studies in Medieval Literature In Honor of Professor Albert Croll Baugh*. Ed. MacEdward Leach. Philadelphia: University of Pennsylvania Press. 187-207.

Spearing, A.C. (1987). *Readings in Medieval Poetry*. Cambridge: Cambridge University Press.

Tester, S.J. (ed.) (1973). *The Consolation of Philosophy*. In *The Theological Tractates*. Loeb Classical Library 74. Cambridge, MA: Harvard University Press, and London: Heinemann.

Ullmann, Walter (1966). *Principles of Government and Politics in the Middle Ages*. 2nd edition. London: Methuen.

Van Schaik, Martin (1988). *De harp in de Middeleeuwen. Studies naar de symboliek van een muziekinstrument*. Utrecht. This study is also available in English: Van Schaik, Martin (1991). *The Harp in the Middle Ages. The Symbolism of a Musical Instrument*. Assen: Van Gorcum.

Veldhoen, Bart (1990). Psychology and the Middle English Romances: Preliminaries to Readings of *Sir Gawain and the Green Knight, Sir Orfeo* and *Sir Launfal*. In: Aertsen and MacDonald, 1990:101-28.

Webb, Clemens C.I. (ed.) (1965). *Ioannis Saresberiensis Episcopi Carnotensis Policratici sive De Nugis Curialium et Vestigiis Philosophorum Libri VIII* Frankfurt a.M.: Minerva. (1st publ. 1909).

THE *ANCRENE WISSE*

JOHAN KERLING
(Alphen aan de Rijn)

The *Ancrene Wisse* (or 'Guide for Anchoresses') was composed by an Augustinian priest some time between 1190 and 1225. An analysis of the language shows that it was written in the West Midlands, close to the Welsh Border, in particular northern Herefordshire or southern Shropshire; indeed, it seems likely that for the origin of the *Ancrene Wisse* we must look to Wigmore Abbey.[1]

The work exists in eight English manuscripts, and in French and Latin translations,[2] the very number of extant manuscripts testifying to the one-time popularity of the work. Of these manuscripts, MS Corpus Christi College Cambridge 402 is usually taken as a basis for discussion since it is probably closest to the original text (now lost). Only the CCCC 402 manuscript bears the contemporary title *Ancrene Wisse*. The lost original is often referred to as *Ancrene Riwle* ("Rule for Anchoresses"), so as to distinguish it from the later text, which is a somewhat expanded version for a larger community. Since none of the other MS versions bears a title, it has now become customary to refer to all versions (except CCCC 402) as *Ancrene Riwle*.

The *Ancrene Wisse* is, as Bennett and Smithers (1968:223) put it, "a manual ... for the guidance of three sisters ... who had become recluses." We do not know the names of the three sisters, and indeed, we do not even know in what sense they were sisters—the word 'sister' may have been used solely in a spiritual sense by the author of the *Ancrene Wisse*. The information available points to the three sisters being the sisters 'living in the Deerfold' to whom Roger de Mortimer had given the chapel of the Blessed Virgin and of St. Leonard (Dobson, 1976:219, 250). However, we know a little more about the circumstances they lived in as this information can be culled from indirect references in the text of the *Ancrene Wisse*.

---

[1] For this and much of the following information, I am indebted to the absorbing study by E.J. Dobson (1976).

[2] For the *stemma codicum*, see Dobson, 1976:287.

Although dictionaries and encyclopaedias often define 'anchorites' and 'anchoresses' as 'hermits', it is preferable to talk about
recluses. As Geoffrey Shepherd (1959:xxx) puts it, "It is usual and
convenient to distinguish as "hermits" those who responded to this
call (that is for a solitary life of contemplation) by a life of devotion
in geographical isolation, from "recluses", those who lived in strict
physical confinement."

This strict physical confinement was achieved by the formal
inclusion of the anchorite or anchoress in a cell attached to a church
or monastery, and during the inclusion-ceremony a mass was celebrated, which could be either one specially written for the occasion
or the regular Mass for the Dead. After all, the anchoress was to live
as one dead to the world, and her house is likened to a grave: *hwet is
ancre hus bute hire burinesse?* (*AW*, 29a/7 [58]; 'What is her anchor-
house but her grave?' [Salu, 47]).[3]

The anchoresses for whom the text was originally written
were probably women of noble birth since they were able to read,
knew French and possibly Latin, and because they could afford to
retreat from the world and keep servants. At some stage in their
lives they must have decided to retreat from the world, but did not
want to become nuns, the difference between a nun and an anchoress
being amongst other things that "an anchoress, unlike a nun, was not
subject to a formal discipline under a monastic superior, but was
required only to vow chastity, stability of place, and obedience to the
bishop or his superiors" (Dobson, 1976: 52). This does not mean that
anchoresses were always rich or of noble birth. In the parish of
Shere (Surrey), Christine, daughter of William the Carpenter, peti-
tioned the bishop of Winchester to be enclosed "in a narrow place in
the churchyard adjoining the parish church" in 1329. The house
where she and her father lived was part of a manor owned by
Richard, son of John, Lord Lieutenant of Ireland.[4]

A reading of the *Ancrene Wisse* gives us a picture of women
living a solitary life in a building attached to a church or chapel. As

[3] All references to the Ancrene Wisse are by folio and line to MS CCCC 402, as
edited for the EETS by Tolkien (1962), with page references to Tolkien's edition
between square brackets. All translations are from Salu (1955).

[4] Christine's career as an anchoress is an interesting one since she was enclosed in
1329, gave up anchoritic life (without permission) and was re-enclosed in 1332
with special consent from the Pope. See *Christine Carpenter: The Anchoress of
Shere*, St. James's Church, Shere, no date. I am indebted to Mrs W. Bijleveld-Six
for this information.

is to be expected, the ultimate reason why these women opted for a solitary life was the expectancy of eternal heavenly bliss, or in the words of the author of the *Ancrene Wisse, ʒe schule beon ihehet iþe blisse of heouene* (*AW*, 46ᵇ/25-6 [90]; 'you shall be raised up in the happiness of heaven' [Salu, 76]). In this they follow—again according to their adviser—the examples of, amongst others, John the Baptist, Christ himself and 'Our dear Lady':

> Vre leoue leafdi ne leadde ha anlich lif? ne fond te engel hire in anli stude al ane? nes ha nowher ute, ah wes biloken feste. for swa we ifindeð: *Ingressus angelus ad eam dixit: Aue Maria gratia plena d'. t. b. tu in ml.* þet is, þe engel wende in to hire. þenne wes heo inne in anli stude hire ane. Engel to mon i þrung ne eadewede neauer ofte. On oðer half þurh þet nowher in hali writ nis iwriten of hire speche bute fowr siðen as is iseid þruppe, sutel prufunge hit is þet ha wes muchel ane þe heold swa silence.   (*AW*, 43ᵇ/11-20)

> (Did not Our dear Lady lead a solitary life? Did not the angel find her in a place of solitude, alone? She was not outside, but was securely enclosed, for we find: *The angel being come in, said unto her: Hail, Mary, full of grace, the Lord is with thee: blessed art thou among women.* At the time when this happened, she was indoors, in a place of solitude, on her own. Seldom has an angel appeared to anyone in the midst of a crowd. And, what is more, because her words are recorded in Holy Scripture only four times, as we have said before, this is clear proof that one who kept such silence must have been often alone. [Salu, 71])

The nature of the spirituality aimed at is thus a very simple one: personal salvation, which can be achieved through personal, physical isolation, through which a better knowledge of oneself and of God can be obtained. This concern with personal salvation and a more intimate knowledge of God is characteristic of new religious developments in the twelfth century, best exemplified by the foundation of the Cistercian order. As Dobson has noted (1976:170), in the *Ancrene Wisse* a strong Cistercian influence can be detected. It is tempting to compare anchoresses with fourteenth-century mystics such as Rolle. Yet, as Shepherd has observed (1959:lvii),

> There is litte point in speaking of AW as a mystical work. Though the work of men like Richard Rolle and

Walter Hilton may indeed owe something in matter as
well as form to the Rule, they are cut off from it by a
reversal in spirituality. The rule is not concerned with
the experience of union with God. ... It follows instead
the earlier Western tradition which regarded the highest
type of life as an intellectual life which yet acknowledged the calls and interruptions of practical business
and acts of social duty and charity.

In other words, where mystics see 'contemplative' life as the
highest ideal, anchorites and anchoresses may be said to have opted
for the 'mixed' life, the other alternative being an exclusively 'active'
life.

They lived in a cell in a house that "was built on to the wall of
the church" (Dobson, 1976:255), and each cell had three windows:
the *parlures þurl*, a window giving on to a reception room so that an
anchoress could speak to any guest without her having to leave her
cell at all; the *huses þurl*, the window through which she could talk
to her servants, and finally the *chirche þurl*, the window through
which she "could see into the church, hear mass said, and receive the
sacrament" (Dobson, 1976: 254).[5] The functions of the three windows are described in the following passage:

Vt þurh þe chirche þurl ne halde ȝe tale wið namon, ah
beo reð þer to wurðmunt for þe hali sacrement þet ȝe
seoð þerþurh. & neomeð oðerwhile to ower wummen þe
huses þurl; to oþre, þe parlur. Speoken ne ahe ȝe bute
ed tes twa þurles.   (*AW*, 17a/18-23 [37])

(Do not hold a conversation with anyone through the church window, but reverence it because of the holy Sacrament which you can
see through it. Use the house window sometimes for speaking to
your women; for other people, that of the parlour. You should not
speak to anyone save at these two windows. [Salu, 30])

However, as this passage already indicates, only sparing use
should be made of the windows, especially of the parlour window.
Anchoresses should talk as little as possible, since

---

[5] I have simplified a problem here: it is not clear whether the three sisters lived in
individual cells or together in a shared room.

Heo grint greot þe chafleð. þe twa cheken beoð ðe twa
grindel stanes. þe tunge is þe cleappe. lokið leoue sustren þet ower cheken ne grinden neauer bute sawle fode.
ne ower eare ne drinke neauer but sawle heale. & nawt
ane ower eare, ah ower ehþurhsperreð to aȝeines idel
speche. to ow ne cume na tale, ne tidinge of þe worlde.
(AW, 17b/15-21)

(A chattering woman is one who is grinding chaff; her two jaws are
the two grindstones, and her tongue is the clapper. Take care, dear
sisters, that your jaws grind only what is nourishing to the soul, and
that your ears drink only those things that will keep the soul healthy;
and secure not only your ears, but also your windows against vain
conversation, letting in no worldly news or gossip. [Salu, 31])

To this end curtains should be made of *þe clað ... twafald.
Blac þet clað, þe cros hwit, wið innen & wið uten* (*AW*, 12b/24-5
[30]; 'two kinds of cloth, a black ground with a white cross showing
both inside and outside' [Salu, 21]). This curtain will also help the
anchoress to avoid peeping out and thus being tempted:

Me wenest tu, seið sum, þet ich wulle leapen on him þah
ich loki on him? Godd wat, leoue suster, mare wunder
ilomp. Eue þi moder leop efter hire ehnen. from þe ehe
to þe eappel. from þe eappel i parais, dun to þer eorðe.
from †e eorðe to helle. þer ha lei i prisun fowr þusent
ȝer & mare, heo & hire were ba. & demde al hire of-
sprung to leapen al efter hire to deað wið uten ende.
Biginnunge & rote of al þis ilke reowðe wes a liht
sihðe. (*AW*, 14ᵃ/3-11 [32])

("But do you think," someone will say, "that I shall leap upon him
because I look at him?" God knows, my dear sister, more surprising
things have happened. Your mother Eve leaped after her eyes had
leapt; from the eye to the apple, from the apple in paradise down to
the earth, and from earth to hell where she remained, in prison, four
thousand years and more, together with her husband, and she con-
demned all her children to leap after her, to endless death. The
beginning and the root of all this misery was a light glance. [Salu,
23])

As the quotations from the *Ancrene Wisse* given above show,
this religious work is livelier in style and content than one would
expect from a manual with so unpromising a title. The instances of

liveliness provided by the quotations above are by no means restricted to these quotations: they are characteristic of the whole
work.

The work is divided into eight parts, the first and the last dealing with the 'outer' rule, as opposed to the 'inner', spiritual rule of
the six parts in between: Devotions; The Custody of the Senses; The
Regulation of the Inward Feelings; Temptations; Confession;
Penance; Love; External Rules.

Each of the eight parts show that the author of the *Ancrene
Wisse* was a man of considerable learning, who knew the Bible and
the writings of the church-fathers, commentaries and exegetical
works. He is in many respects a typical medieval clergyman, who
doctrinally stays well within the bounds of medieval ecclesiastical
tradition and thinking, and who shares the beliefs of his audience.

However, in each of the eight parts into which the work is
divided, and especially in the first and the eighth, we get the impres-
sion not only of a man of considerable learning, but also of one
whose main concern was the physical and spiritual well-being of the
three sisters, and who insisted that *best is eauer mete* (*A W*, 78ª/23
[148]; 'moderation is always best' [Salu, 127]). Therefore it does not
come a a surprise to find him telling the anchoresses that the inner
rule *is eauer & an wið uten changunge* (AW, 1ᵇ/28 [7]; '... does not
vary' [Salu, 2]), but that the outer rule

> ... changin hire misliche. efter euchanes manere & efter
> hire euene. for sum is strong, sum unstrong & mei ful
> wel beo cwite & paie Godd mid leasse. Sum is clergesse,
> sum nawt & [mot te] mare wurchen & on oðer wise
> seggen hire bonen. Sum is ald & eðelich & is þe leasse
> dred of. Sum is ȝung & luuelich & is neod betere
> warde.   (*A W*, 2ª/9-15 [7-8])

> (... may be changed in various ways according to the circumstances
> and abilities of each anchoress; for whereas one person is strong,
> another is delicate and may very well be excused from some things,
> and may please God with less; one person reads and studies,
> another cannot, and must do more work of other kinds, and say her
> prayers without books; one is young and fair and needs to be more
> guarded than another who is old and who more easily passes unob-
> served, and for whom there is so much the less danger. [Salu, 2-3])

This preference for moderation and this humane attitude are
found throughout the work, as, for instance, when the author says

that *Al þet ich habbe iseid of flesches pinsunge nis nawt for ow, mine leoue sustren, þe oðerhwile þolieð mare þen ich walde* (*AW*, 102b/ 13-15 [193]; 'all that I have said about mortification of the flesh is not intended for you, my dear sisters, who sometimes suffer more than I would have you' [Salu, 167]), or *noðeles, leoue sustren, ower mete ant ower drunch haueð iþuht me ofte leasse þen ich walde. Ne feaste ȝe na dei to bread ne to weattre, bute ȝe habben leaue* (*AW*, 111b/17-20 [211]; 'and yet, dear sisters, your food and drink have often seemed to me less than I should like you to have. Do not, on any day, fast on bread and water unless you have permission' [Salu, 183]). Likewise he tells them

> Nest lich nan ne gurde hire wið na cunne gurdles, bute þurh schriftes leaue. ne beore nan irn ne here, ne ilespiles felles, ne ne beate hire þer wið, ne wið scurge ileadet, wið holin ne wið breres, ne biblodgi hire seolf, wið ute schriftes leaue.   (*AW*, 113b/2-6 [214])

> (Let no one wear a belt of any kind next to the skin except by her confessor's permission, or wear anything made of iron or hair or hedgehog-skins, or discipline herself with anything made of these, or with a leaded scourge, or with holly or thorns, or draw blood from her body, without her confessor's permission. [Salu, 185-6])

The author shows a liking for proverbs and statements with a proverbial ring about them: *ofte a ful haher smið smeoðeð a ful wac cnif. þe wise folhe i wisdom, & nawt i folie* (*AW*, 13b/2-3 [31]; 'a very skilful smith often produces a very poor knife; follow the wise in their wisdom, and not in their folly' [Salu, 22]) and, *se þe hul is herre, se þe wind is mare þron* (*AW*, 47b/24-5 [92]; 'the higher the hill the more the wind blows about it' [Salu, 78]). His frequent similes are often drawn from real-life situations, thus giving us glimpses of the social life of the period:

> Efter ower sunnen, hwen se ȝe þencheð of helle wa & of heoue-riches wunnen, understondeð þet Godd walde o sum wise schawin ham to men i þis world bi worltliche pinen & worltliche wunnen, & schaweð ham forð as schadewe; for na lickre ne beoð ha to þe wunne of heouene ne to þe wa of helle þen is schadewe to þet þing þet hit is of schadewe. Ȝe beoð ouer þis worldes sea, up o þe brugge of heouene: lokið þet ȝe ne beon nawt þe

hors eschif iliche, þe schuncheð for a schadewe & falleð
adun i þe weater of þe hehe brugge. To childene ha beoð
þe fleoð a peinture þe þuncheð ham grislich & grureful
to bihalden: wa & wunne i þis world—al nis bute peint-
unge, al nis bute schadewe.   (*AW*, 65ª/26-65ᵇ/9 [123-4])

(After you have meditated on your sins and are thinking of the pains
of hell and the joys of heaven, remember that God wants to make
them in a sort known to people here on earth through earthly pains
and earthly joys, but that He is only shadowing them forth, for they
are no more like the actual joys of heaven or the actual pains of hell
than a shadow is like the object of which it is the shadow. You are
upon the bridge of heaven, up above the sea of this world. See that
you are not like a nervous horse, shying at a shadow and falling
from the high bridge down into the water. They are too childish who
run away from a painting which strikes them with terror. Pain and
joy in this world are the merest painting, shadows simply. [Salu,
107])

Þe Seste confort is þet ure lauerd hwen he þoleð þet we
beon itemptet, he pleieð wið us as þe moder wið hire
ʒunge deorling. flið from him & hut hire. & let him
sitten ane. & lokin ʒeorne abuten cleopien dame, dame.
& wepen ane hwile. & þenne wið spredde earmes leapeð
lahhinde forð, cluppeð & cusseð & wipeð his ehnen.
                                        (*AW*, 62ᵇ/6-12 [118-19])

(The sixth comfort is that our Lord, when He allows us to be
tempted, is playing with us as a mother with her darling child. She
runs away from him and hides, and leaves him on his own, and he
looks around for her, calling "Mama! Mama!" and crying a little,
and then she runs out to him quickly, her arms outspread, and she
puts them round him, and kisses him, and wipes his eyes. [Salu,
102])

Likewise the use of bestiaries is characteristic of him: he does
not shy away from the use of this popular material. Thus in Part III
on the 'Regulation of the Inward Feelings' we find that true anchoresses are likened to *briddes ..., for ha leaueð þe eorðe, þet is, þe luue
of alle worltliche þinges, &, þurh ʒirnunge of heorte to heouenliche
þinges, fleoð uppart toward heouene* (*AW*, 35ᵇ/22-5 [69]; 'birds ...
because they leave the earth, that is, the love of all worldly things,
and, because of the longing of their hearts towards heavenly things,
fly upward towards heaven' [Salu, 58]), and the bird-images used are
those of the pelican, ostrich, eagle, night-bird and sparrow. In Part

IV on 'Temptations' the seven deadly sins are also given their traditional likenesses to animals, but these are animals of the ground: here we find *Liun of prude. Neddre of attri onde. Vnicorne of wreaððe. Beore of dead slawðe. Vox of ȝisceunge. Suhe of ȝiuernesse. Scorpiun wið þe teil of stinginde leccherie, þet is galnesse* (AW, 52a/21-4 [101]; 'the Lion of Pride, the Serpent of venomous Envy, the Unicorn of Wrath, the Bear of deadly Sloth, the Fox of Covetousness, the Sow of Gluttony, the Scorpion with its tail of stinging Lechery, that is lust' [Salu, 86]).

As a typical medieval writer he also makes grateful use of allegory, as, for example, when Christ is likened to the king who so much loved a destitute lady in an earthen castle. The disdainful lady, although accepting his help, refused to love him. The author of the *Ancrene Wisse* continues

Ah swa, þurh his deboneirte, luue hefde ouercumen him, þet he seide on ende: Dame, þu art iweorret & þine van beoþ se stronge þet tu ne maht nanesweis wið ute mi sucurs edfleon hare honden, þet ha ne don þe to scheome deað efter al þin weane. Ich chulle, for þe luue of þe, neome þet feht up o me & arudde þe of ham þe þi deað secheð, Ich wat þah to soðe þet ich schal bituhen ham neomen deaðes wunde; & ich hit wulle heorteliche forte ofgan þin heorte. Nu þenne biseche ich þe, for þe luue þet ich cuðe þe, þet tu luuie me lanhure after ilke dede, dead, hwan þu naldest, liues. Þes king dude al þus: arudde hire of ale hire van & wes him seolf to wundre ituket & islein on ende; þurh miracle aras þah from deaðe to liue. Nere þeos ilke leafdi of uueles cunnes cunde, ȝef ha ouer alle þing ne luuede him her efter?

Þes king is Iesu, Godes sune, þet al o þisse wise wohede ure sawle þe deoflen hefden biset.

(AW, 105^b/6-22 [199])

(But love had so vanquished his tender heart, that at last he said, "Lady, thou art assailed, and thine enemies are so strong that thou canst by no means escape their hands without my help, which can prevent their putting thee to a shameful death after all thy misery. For love of thee I will take this fight upon myself and deliver thee from those who seek thy death. I know without any doubt that among them I must receive my death-wound, but I will meet it gladly in order to win thy heart. Now I beseech thee, for the love I show thee, that thou shouldst love me, at least after my death has been accomplished, who wouldst not while I lived." The king carried out all this, delivered her from all her enemies, and was himself outrageously tortured and finally slain. But by a miracle he rose from death to life. Would not this lady be of an evil nature had she not loved him thereafter beyond everything else?

This king is Jesus, the Son of God, who in just this way sought our soul's love when it was besieged by devils.[Salu, 172-3])

There can be no doubt, in my opinion, that this liveliness, this down-to-earth attitude, this direct style and no-nonsense matter-of-factness places the *Ancrene Wisse* firmly, and as a prime example, in the medieval English vernacular sermon-tradition: the *Ancrene Wisse* exemplifies "as far as a vernacular tradition can, the aims, tone, manner of address, and the verbal devices generally approved in sermon writing at the beginning of the thirteenth century" (Shepherd, 1959:lx). For this reason it is taking things too far to say, as Bennett and Smithers do, that the "dogma that the *Ancrene Riwle* is a main example of the 'continuity' of Old and Middle English prose is thus a major error of literary history" (1968:224). If, as they say, "the author's warm, intimate, easy tone and his conversational syntax are as novel in our prose as his apparatus of style" (1968:224), this does not mean that he is therefore automatically outside the continuing prose tradition of Old and Middle English. He is merely outside the one particular homiletic tradition which carried on the patterns set by Aelfric, and, to some extent, by Wulfstan, in the late tenth and early eleventh centuries. This tradition is broadly characterized by a dependence on the rhythms and alliteration of Old English poetry, and to a lesser extent on standardized diction. As Dorothy Bethurum says (1935:556),

> ... there is wanting in the *Ancrene Riwle* the regular use of alliteration which is so characteristic a feature of the saints' lives. The work belongs, it is true, to the general English tradition of devotional prose, and that means that it uses the adornments of poetry freely; but in a strict sense it may justly be said that the *Riwle* is unique up to this point in its independence both of the ornate prose of the late Old English period and of the common Latin models for vernacular writing ...

The prose style of the *Ancrene Wisse* is characterized by a conversational ease that owes little to the stylistic devices of poetry.

It is prose that is based on the syntax and speech rhythms of every-day speech, and thus continues a tradition the foundation of which was laid by Alfred in the ninth century.

The *Ancrene Wisse*, then, belongs to a prose tradition that also produced some of the best English sermons, and which ultimately proved the strongest since it was closes to the spoken language. The tradition was kept up by writers such as Wyclif and Malory, and eventually led to what Gordon (1966:120ff) calls the speech-based prose of the seventeenth and eighteenth centuries, the period in which the pattern was set for all later English prose. This, and the author's humaneness, coupled with his down-to-earth attitude and his sense of humour account for the fact that the *Ancrene Wisse* remains one of the most enjoyable instances of Middle English prose writing.

REFERENCES

Bennett, J.A.W. and G.V. Smithers (eds.) (1968). *Early Middle English Verse and Prose*. 2nd ed. Oxford: Oxford University Press. (1st ed., 1966).
Bethurum, Dorothy (1935). The Connection of the Katherine Group with Old English Prose. *Journal of English and Germanic Philology* 34. 553-64.
Dobson, E.J. (1976). *The Origins of* Ancrene Wisse. Oxford: Oxford University Press.
Gordon, Ian A. (1966). *The Movement of English Prose*. London: Longmans.
Salu, M.B. (trans.) (1955). *The Ancrene Riwle*. London: Burns and Oates. (Repr. 1990. Exeter: University of Exeter Press).
Shepherd, Geoffrey (ed.) (1959). *Ancrene Wisse: Parts Six and Seven*. London and Edinburgh: Nelson. (Repr. 1972. Manchester: Manchester University Press).
Tolkien, J.R.R. (ed.) (1962). *The English Text of the* Ancrene Riwle: Ancrene Wisse. *Edited from MS. Corpus Christi College Cambridge 402*. EETS, 249.